Shift Teaching Forward

Shift Teaching Forward

Advancing Career Skills to Prepare Tomorrow's Workforce

Kelly Cassaro
with Dana Lee

JB JOSSEY-BASS™
A Wiley Brand

Published by John Wiley & Sons, Inc., Hoboken, New Jersey.
Published simultaneously in Canada.

For general information on our other products and services or for technical support, please contact our Customer Care Department within the United States at (800) 762-2974, outside the United States at (317) 572-3993 or fax (317) 572-4002.

Wiley also publishes its books in a variety of electronic formats. Some content that appears in print may not be available in electronic formats. For more information about Wiley products, visit our web site at www.wiley.com.

Library of Congress Cataloging-in-Publication Data is Available:

ISBN 9781119900207 (Paperback)
ISBN 9781119900221 (ePub)
ISBN 9781119900214 (ePDF)

Cover Design: Paul McCarthy
Cover Art: © Getty Images | Pepifoto

SKY10063708_010224

This book is dedicated to my grandfather Vincenzo (James) Pesce who always taught us to find a career you love, no matter what. He didn't believe that one job was "better" than another. He believed that "you" were the ingredient that mattered. If you worked as hard as you could and strived to achieve at high levels, you could find true fulfillment in life and earn a living to support your family.

He likely felt this way because after he served in World War II, he wanted, with all his heart, to take advantage of the GI Bill and become a teacher. However, he felt he couldn't go to school because he needed to support his non-English speaking immigrant parents. He instead "apprenticed" for free until he was good enough to be hired as a welder at a Pittsburgh ship building company and, over time, became a foreman at the same company, leading a team of over 100.

He taught me that education and hard work can change your life. And it has for me.

Thanks, Pap.

Contents

Shift Teaching Forward

Introduction

Even as a child, I knew teaching was the most important job on Earth. At age five, I declared that I was going to be a teacher. I never wavered.

As I continued my education, my belief in the power of education to change lives only strengthened. I have found joy and both personal and professional progress through the skills and knowledge that education offered to me: escaping to another place with a good book, overcoming a lack of confidence by learning to crisply defend an argument, building community by working together with peers to accomplish a goal, and opening doors to global travel through my work in supporting career trainings around the world.

Everyone on Earth deserves meaningful education and the transformative impact it has on one's life. As well, everyone on Earth deserves the dignity and security that come from sustaining, satisfying employment. The link between the two is solid—even as the landscape of career opportunities shifts before our eyes, ever more quickly as the speed of technological advancement refuses to slow down. Demand for some of the 20th century's most steady, reliable jobs continues to fizzle out while many of today's in-demand jobs didn't even exist when I was in school.

The most seasoned educators may find it daunting to connect educational experiences of today with the unknown, often mysterious job and career marketplace of tomorrow. No one has a crystal ball. Yet, educators and trainers must design learning experiences as if they do. This is no small feat, but it can be done.

After all, excellent educators have made the impossible possible for ages. The current moment is no different. Some jobs of the future may not yet exist, but educators and trainers can still make an incredible impact right now on their learners' future employability. Educators and trainers understand the value of education and want doors of opportunity flung wide open for students, especially in our rapidly changing post-pandemic world. And this means they'll do everything they can to see around corners and guide their learners toward successful careers—both with new strategies and with traditional, tried-and-true methods applied in new ways.

That is what *Shift Teaching Forward* is all about—equipping educators and trainers with the rationale and know-how to guide their practice so they can better prepare learners for the world of work in which they'll one day thrive.

Shift Teaching Forward offers practical strategies to bridge the gap between education and employment. This book is intended for all educators and trainers who support learners in preparing for a career: teachers, designers, administrators, and nonprofit leaders within a variety of settings, including high schools, vocational schools, community-based programs, colleges, universities, and corporations.

My teaching journey has spanned early childhood to adult education. The lessons I have learned through those varied experiences throughout the years have had me continuously saying, "I wish I had known that when I was in the classroom." My first teaching position in the South Bronx, New York, was in a third-grade classroom with students from Ghana and Gambia, and some did not yet speak English fluently. While we did read amazing books together and learn about history, art, and geography, there was a laser focus on standardized tests; any discussions about the future stopped at high school graduation/college admissions. While the educators sometimes had cross-grade professional development, the pressure and intensity were on meeting urgent, tested curricular requirements. The immediate application of learnings from other grade levels was not clear. The mandate to cover standards for third grade was, however, abundantly clear.

I continued as a classroom teacher for seven years and added kindergarten and first-grade teaching to my résumé. I fell in love with teaching and, at the same time, realized the cruel realities facing educators in the United States. I felt compelled to experience other roles within the sector and aimed to position myself to influence change. After classroom teaching, I've held positions ranging from leading professional development for a network of schools, leading recruitment of teachers, driving the overall academic program, creating curriculum for adult education, and leading a global team of educators in pursuit of developing programs and methodologies to support adults into meaningful employment that can change their lives.

Although I have held many roles within the field of education, the first seven years in the classroom were certainly the most challenging. I gave my all to improving my craft to better serve my students. I poured a lot into my students and left little for myself. I know you do the same.

I know these are the contexts you bring with you when reading a book like this. You're hungry for ideas, strategies, and inspiration, and you need to be able to bring all that into your own classroom, training center, or virtual video conference. You know the world is changing, and your learners need to be ready for whatever comes next. That doesn't change the reality in which you do your work, day in and day out.

The challenges I faced—the same that I see so many of my peers, friends, and family continue to face—only strengthened my resolve to improve others' lives, especially the lives of teachers. I often consider a speech from Pulitzer Prize winner Anna Quindlen, who's had a long and rewarding career as an author. She noted, "Teachers are the second most powerful group of people in your life. A teacher said to me, 'You are a writer' in a way that was undeniable, and it shaped my entire future." If you are holding this book (thank you!), chances are you hold the same awesome power as that teacher held for Ms. Quindlen—the power to support a student in shaping their life's trajectory. You have the power to ensure your teaching is transformational instead of transactional. You have the power to form partnerships with the community, seize opportunities, and foster the curiosities and talents of students. You have the power to prepare them for a thriving career—even if neither you, nor them, has any idea what shape that career will take.

You have the power to make a powerful mindset shift away from what has long been known and established—that college prep is the core role of K–12 learning, and that the best employment pathways involve predictable and well-trodden paths. This shift requires opening your mind to the role of career preparation no matter the context in which you teach, embracing the integration of employability and social-emotional learning skills in daily classroom life, and choosing optimism in the face of incredible uncertainty and technological change. It's a big shift, especially when so much of your role already requires you to go above and beyond any job description in print. Yet it's a needed shift that will bring joy and marketable skills to your learners.

Over the past seven years, I've had the great privilege of traveling the world to see adult training in action. The settings have ranged from employer-embedded training programs, massive government training initiatives, and smaller, community-based initiatives. I've sat alongside workers, shoulder-to-shoulder, and witnessed a variety of professions in action, including stitching-machine operators in Pakistan, construction helpers in Texas, and disability support workers in Australia. These hands-on experiences have offered me an understanding of the day in and day out of many professions, including the common threads that run through roles that seemingly would not have much in common. I have spoken to countless employers about what makes a high-performing employee and have been able to pull out trends applicable across sectors. I am also fortunate that through these varied experiences, I have learned from the most incredible colleagues. Through these experiences, I've collected learnings and strategies to support educators in the incredible responsibility of preparing learners to thrive in their careers and, more broadly, their lives.

My experiences have given me insights into what students need from their education in order to succeed in our rapidly changing workplace. I have witnessed our current education system transforming student lives, but I have also observed and studied the gaps between what our students' current education offers them and what they need to thrive in the workplace. In 2018, Ralph Wolff and Melanie Booth, then both senior leaders of The Quality Assurance Commons for Higher and Postsecondary Education, asserted how "Employer surveys consistently reveal that more than disciplinary knowledge and skills is needed to be successful in today's workplace—regardless of the field, level of education, or level of work" and that "what have traditionally been called 'soft skills' have in fact become essential employability qualities" (Wolff & Booth, 2017, p. 52). In other words, you'll need more than technical skills to land that new job, and the "soft skills" that once were icing on the cake are now undeniably indispensable.

This should give trainers and educators hope. A crystal ball isn't necessary if the actual technical skills needed to succeed are only part of the equation. From my early days teaching social-emotional skills in elementary school to my recent work teaching the same skills to adults, I've seen firsthand how these valuable life skills can be appropriately taught and reinforced to give learners an incredible advantage toward career and life success.

In this book, we'll dive into what these future-proof skills are, their demonstrated impact, how to evaluate programming that supports them, and how to integrate these skills and the world of work into your classroom or training center. We'll do this after evaluating the current landscape—and its expected changes—as well as the evolving role of education in preparation for these changes.

There will be naysayers who see the focus on non-technical aspects of career readiness as a distraction at best or waste of time at worst. This can easily be exacerbated by a school or program's intense focus on external-mandated academic standards or standardized testing. In a training setting outside of the K–12 system, it can be similarly easy to defer to technical skills first. I've often heard from expert and well-intentioned program coordinators, "We don't have time for that soft stuff—there's too much actual skills content we need to do first."

As real as these attitudes and requirements are, and as aggressive as course syllabi and training curricula can be, educators and trainers must not turn a blind eye to the growing movement and body of research showing just how essential the "soft stuff" is. The ever-shifting workplace and our societal understanding of "work" is different now than it was even 10 years ago. Sticking with just one profession, or even one company, throughout your entire career is no longer common. Even while writing this book, generative Artificial Intelligence (AI) had a breakthrough, bringing even more attention to technology's disruptive innovations in the workplace.

Throughout this book, we will examine the challenges and roadblocks faced by students when determining their career path, as well as challenges faced by the teachers who act as shepherds along their journey. You will have an opportunity to dig into strategies and approaches that work to alleviate these challenges. With so much changing, educators who equip their students with the enduring knowledge, skills, and aptitudes that foster success no matter the circumstances will have tremendous impact on the next generation of job seekers. This book will give you the head start you need to embrace this shift and get started on the work.

First, I will establish a foundational understanding of how the workplace is evolving and why a shift is necessary in how we prepare learners. Then, we'll look at the core knowledge, skills, and aptitudes that give students a universal advantage even for roles that don't yet exist. Finally, we'll dig into resources and strategies to evaluate program effectiveness, bring the world of work into your classroom, and bridge the gap between education and successful employment. Each chapter ends with reflection questions and intentions to support application to your own context.

Throughout the book, "Spotlight Stories" will highlight strategies in action across various teaching contexts to help make connections to your own professional situation. Because this work is deeply personal to me, I'll also share my own experiences in sections noted as "From the Personal Archive." Through these anecdotes and vignettes, I hope to breathe additional life into the experiences, research, and shifts covered throughout the book.

Unfortunately, many people in our society do not respect and honor teachers and their unique and distinct abilities. It seems too often that those who've never taught are the ones with the loudest advice. That's one reason why I wrote this book as a top-up to the incredible work already being done by educators on the ground, closest to the learners—the ones who live the work every day. I have been where you are and I know how time consuming it is to teach full time, without a single break through the day, all while taking care of mounting personal responsibilities outside of work. To then try to stay up to date with Future of Work research, the jobs landscape, and in-demand career skills feels like yet another unfair expectation.

As my career evolved, I kept thinking that I was constantly learning things I wished I'd known as a classroom teacher. I saw a gap for teachers and trainers, and I hope this book will help fill this gap—that through it, educators continue to serve as sage advocates for learners with a sharper eye toward preparing for future employment. I want this book to save you the time of synthesizing this for yourself. I aim to provide research-backed context, heartfelt encouragement, and actionable ideas to shift teaching forward toward meaningful support of student career paths. If any teacher or trainer feels better equipped, through their own actions and choices, to create lifelong learners who are ready to nourish careers that are aligned to their skills and interests, I'll count this text a success.

When you apply these comprehensive principles and strategies, you will help your students achieve personal fulfillment. As with any worthwhile endeavor, transforming your approach and best practices will take time. You'll need to do the work of applying the learnings to your context. However, it will be worthwhile work.

I have faced challenges in my career. Maybe you can relate to some—loads of student debt, limited resources with which to engage learners, the negative social stigma sometimes attributed to George Bernard Shaw that, "those who can't do, teach." Yet, to this day, I wake up with a fire to keep going and tackle the newest challenges. I want others to nurture that same fire in educators and trainers. I want to support them so that they can feel the satisfaction that comes from reaching their personal and professional goals. I want to partner with others who are called to make sure that today's learners are ready for the dawn that's breaking tomorrow.

Educators, trainers, administrators, leaders—know that I see you. I see you up late working, spending your own hard-earned money on your classroom or training program, working tirelessly for your students. Let me help you move forward to scalable and enduring results. It is my sincere hope that through my varied educational experiences, knowledge of the Future of Work across professional sectors, and understanding of cutting-edge educational practices, you will be able to tweak, augment, and supplement your practice to truly shift your teaching forward.

Reflections and Intentions

- Consider your own path to identifying a career. What came easily to you? What roadblocks did you overcome? What supports did you have?
- How does your current educational or training program consider the big picture of the lifelong learning and career journey?
- Think about one student who faces big challenges identifying or navigating their career path; internally dedicate the time you will spend working through this book to them and their journey.

1 The Jobs Landscape Is Changing

"Employers estimate that 44% of workers' skills will be disrupted in the next five years. Cognitive skills are reported to be growing importance most quickly, reflecting the increasing importance of complex problem-solving in the workplace."

—"The Future of Jobs Report 2023" by the World Economic Forum

I must admit—it feels quite daunting to hear people talk about the "Future of Work." Teachers feel the weight of their students' unknowable futures every time someone quips, "It will be here before you know it," or "It'll be wildly different than anything we've ever seen before!" "Future of Work" workshops try to lure teachers in with promises of being let into the secrets, although sometimes these promises lack novelty, substance, or both. Educators are left with a riddle to solve—here's an unknown timeline with unknown characteristics, and it's up to you. Better get your students ready!

No one was referring to this phenomenon as the "Future of Work" when I was little, but I remember being inundated with promises of the future and how it would be the total opposite of the present day. I grew up watching reruns of *The Jetsons*—a classic cartoon from the 1960s about a family living in the distant future, enjoying the benefits promised by technological advancement. Recently, I learned that George Jetson's birthday was July 31, 2022. According to the show, flying cars, robot maids, and motorized "slidewalks" were just around the corner, ready to transform our daily lives. While the world is still waiting for those innovations to become everyday items, there have been both incremental and monumental shifts that have made and will continue to make an impact, shifts that we need to be ready for today and tomorrow.

So, what are these shifts? What can we, as educators, do now so that our students are not left behind? How can we make the classroom look more like the world our students will enter? What are the skills that artificial intelligence (AI) and robots cannot perform that our students can? How can we teach the skills that employers are already asking for now (let alone for the future)?

To answer these questions and myriad others, let's first ground our thinking in recent workplace trends and changes before looking to the future.

Change Is the Only Constant

Just a casual exploration into the text-generating world of ChatGPT is enough to send your imagination running. ChatGPT, if you have yet to explore it, is an AI chatbot developed by OpenAI. It allows you to have human-like conversations, including generated suggestions, ideas, and even original compositions. If computers can write poetry, give relationship advice, and program their own Java code, what will be left for us humans to do? This application of AI might not be a robot maid, but it does feel like George Jetson would know exactly how to respond to it.

But technological advancements like this are at once cutting edge and a tale as old as time. The technology itself is new, but humans living through a season of disruptive innovation is not. While sustaining innovation improves existing models, machines, and systems, disruptive innovation changes the entire situation. Consider agricultural practices before the advent of modern machines. Quite likely, farmers were constantly looking for unbreakable tools, or better timelines for sowing seed and harvesting plants. Stronger plows, deeper water wells, birthing more children to secure future farmhands—these enhancements all helped increase outcomes . . . marginally. Then came modern machinery. The cotton gin, the mechanical reaper, and tractors with combustion engines are just a few of the disruptive innovations that dramatically changed the face of modern farming.

Where sustaining innovations improve on ways of doing and being that are familiar and comfortable, disruptive innovations can feel like you're swimming in a whole new ocean, unsure which way is up.

The good news is disruptive innovation isn't new. Collectively, our ancestors endured disruption after disruption to bring each of us to the present moment.

- There was a time when humans subsisted as hunters and gathers. Then came agriculture.
- There was a time when most humans lived, worked, and died on farms. Then came industrialization.
- There was a time when transportation was powered by animals alone. Then came planes, trains, and automobiles.
- There was a time when women had precious few options for work outside their home. Then came the late-20th century.

I don't share this to diminish the tremendous and disruptive changes we're living through today. To be sure, we are living through interesting times, and the unknowns are many. I share this here to remind myself and others that the human race has adapted before, and we'll do it again. And, our ability to demonstrate adaptability and resilience during times of change is worth more than half the battle.

In fact, we've already been adapting as the world of work has been actively evolving in our lifetimes. Even the most veteran of educators still teaching today likely has little memory of life before there were computers in every school—a reality that would have been unthinkable to educators 10 or 20 years more senior. When we shift our default reaction to disruptive innovation away from fear and anxiety and toward curiosity and optimism, new possibilities can emerge that can change lives for the better.

Even before the impact of the global pandemic that began in 2020, technological revolution was unfolding in the labor market before our eyes.

- Manufacturing jobs have steadily declined since the early 1980s. Dropping from a peak of 19.4 million jobs in 1979, a mere 11.5 million such jobs were on record in early 2010. This coincides with a drop in manufacturing's share of the overall workforce. Where almost a third (32.1%) of American workers were in the manufacturing sector in 1953, only 8.5% still are today. Despite output growing due to technological advancements, the decreased opportunities in this type of work can be felt acutely by job hunters looking for entry level options (DeSilver, 2020).
- In the 1970s, the word processor changed offices everywhere. Its successor, the personal computer, wasn't far behind in the 1980s. As the affordability of computers improved in the decades

that followed, modern computing was at everyone's fingertips. Offices gladly gave up manual edits on typewritten pages and bulky filing cabinets filled with documents in need of meticulous organization.

- The internet changed everything. From commerce to research to social connections, the internet is one of most disruptive innovations in recent history. It has enabled workers to work remotely and virtually, creating distributed, even global, teams and organizations that could not have existed this easily in the 20th century. The number of workers who were able to work from home increased by 173% between 2003 and 2018—well before the pandemic upended so many lives (Global Workplace Analytics, n.d.).

Technology has never stopped advancing; we should expect the rest of our lives to be no different. Some jobs will fade away, some will grow, and some will emerge brand-new to us all. Figure 1.1 shows which roles are expected to trend up and down in the coming years.

From Figure 1.1, we see job growth on the left fueled by the same disruptive technologies that are driving decline in the roles to the right.

Fastest growing versus fastest declining jobs

WORLD ECONOMIC FORUM

	Top 10 fastest growing jobs		Top 10 fastest declining jobs
1.	AI and Machine Learning Specialists	1.	Bank Tellers and Related Clerks
2.	Sustainability Specialists	2.	Postal Service Clerks
3.	Business Intelligence Analysts	3.	Cashiers and Ticket Clerks
4.	Information Security Analysts	4.	Data Entry Clerks
5.	Fintech Engineers	5.	Administrative and Executive Secretaries
6.	Data Analysts and Scientists	6.	Material-Recording and Stock-Keeping Clerks
7.	Robotics Engineers	7.	Accounting, Bookkeeping and Payroll clerks
8.	Electrotechnology Engineers	8.	Legislators and Officials
9.	Agricultural Equipment Operators	9.	Statistical, Finance and Insurance Clerks
10.	Digital Transformation Specialists	10.	Door-To-Door Sales Workers, News and Street Vendors, and Related Workers

Note
The jobs which survey respondents expect to grow most quickly from 2023 to 2027 as a fraction of present employment figures

Figure 1.1: Fastest growing versus fastest declining jobs.
Source: World Economic Forum.

As an educator, looking at this information can help us in a variety of ways, such as handing an interested student a book or website on the fast-growing topics or inviting community members within the roles or sector into the classroom. You will find out about more strategies within this book and also some of the employability or 21st-century skills that are essential in virtually any workplace.

The Pandemic and Everything After

No conversation about the changing jobs landscape is complete with acknowledging the profound impact of the Covid-19 global pandemic. The massive disruption to daily life was a new and utterly unwelcome experience for millions of people worldwide, let alone the pain and suffering endured by those who lost loved ones or continue to endure the virus's physical effects.

Layoffs abounded, and restructuring and reorganizations did, too. How we did our work shifted, as did who did the work.

- Industries everywhere shifted to remote work. Employees and teams met goals and stayed connected via video conferences, messaging apps, and collaborative documents. In some industries and companies, this proved viable in the long term; employees now remain either fully remote or working in a hybrid situation (some days in the office, some days at home). Some industries proved how critically important it was to be in person for work—K–12 education leading the list.
- The need to stay physically distant from each other while conducting core functions of life accelerated existing trends toward automation. Banks, grocery stores, entertainment venues, and more all adapted to increase safety and keep doors open.
- Women were disproportionately harmed by the pandemic's impact on the economy and jobs market. Many women were forced to stay home with children whose schooling happened remotely, and some of those women have not yet returned to the workforce—despite schools resuming (mostly) normal functions. Regarding job loss between February 2020 and February 2022, women account for 68.5% of that statistic (National Women's Law Center, 2022).

We're still not out of the woods. Collectively, social scientists and economists will continue to investigate and analyze the pandemic's impact on our economies for decades. In the meantime, educators and trainers will continue to do the work of preparing flexible, adaptable, and desirable talent for the workforce of tomorrow.

Understanding the Future of Work

Ask three professional peers to define the *Future of Work*, and you'll likely get three different answers. And that's okay. For our purposes together, I define the *Future of Work* as follows:

> *The* Future of Work *refers to the changes we expect to see in the global workforce in upcoming years—changes like how people work, where they work, and, of course, the work itself. It considers current and expected advancements in technology, in globalization, and in what we expect from employees and employers. It acknowledges the disruptions we anticipate from artificial intelligence (AI), robotics, digitization, and automation; it also acknowledges the pressing need to rethink how we prepare people for employment and transform education systems to respond to rapid change.*

It is impossible for educators to have a deep understanding of all factors influencing the Future of Work—just think about all job sectors our students may one day pursue! A deep understanding of common human skills that empower a student to thrive, however, is essential: resilience, adaptability, problem solving, adaptive communication, and judgment, for example, are indispensable in the ever-changing workplace of today and tomorrow.

Jamie Casap, Google's Educational Evangelist, works with school districts and other educational organizations to leverage technology to drive innovation for learning. He notes that education needs to be "Preparing students for jobs that don't exist and to use technologies, sciences, and methods that we haven't even discovered yet, to solve problems that we haven't identified" (Gaulden & Gottlieb, 2017). That's a tall order—perhaps impossible—if it weren't for the essential human skills that run constant through that intense list of unknowns.

Who does the work	How the work is done	When and where the work is done
Full-time/part-time employees	AI	Fluid work schedules
Crowdsourcing	Robotics	Remote workers
Gig workers	Automation	Collocated workspace

Figure 1.2: The Future of Work.

Source: "What is Meant by "the Future of Work"? SHRM, 2022, `https://www.shrm.org/resourcesandtools/tools-and-samples/hr-qa/pages/what-is-meant-by-the-future-of-work.aspx`

Before tackling those essential human skills, let's aim to understand the elements involved in the Future of Work. Figure 1.2 uses simple language and straightforward concepts to help demystify the topic. Visualizations like this level the playing field and combat the feeling that only those who are expert in emerging technology and artificial intelligence can unlock career secrets for students. The Society for Human Resource Management (SHRM), an organization whose publications and website have helped me much in navigating all things human resources through the years, has a helpful framework for considering the Future of Work (SHRM, 2022).

They categorize the Future of Work in three ways: (1) who does the work, (2) how the work is done, and (3) when and where the work is done. This framework is helpful when trying to understand something vague and unknown—like a particular role or industry that is of interest to a learner, educator, or trainer. Figure 1.2 outlines the three categories and the components each contains.

Breaking the Future of Work into these categories helps us think about the skills that students might need to be successful within these ways of working. It also can encourage us to verbalize these connections with students. For example, during the pandemic, many families felt the pain of children and teens taking classes online that were designed to be delivered in person. Endless screen time, decreased engagement, and general frustrations led to many unsatisfied learners and educators. But even as my own children stayed home and our family adapted to this form of school, I used this visual to remind myself that my kids were building muscles that could one day serve them well if they work remotely and need to manage fluid work schedules.

Who Does the Work

SHRM notes three categories to describe who does the work of the future: full-time/part-time employees, crowdsourcing, and gig workers. Some educators may be surprised to see employees categorized this way. They may see employment as a dichotomy that's either full time or part time, or perhaps salaried or hourly. Those differences still exist, but now, the expansion of crowdsourcing and gig workers cannot be ignored.

Gig workers may complete small, discrete tasks or bigger, more complex jobs. With crowdsourcing, companies can get inputs, data, or ideas from large groups of people who gather in one place virtually—for example, consider a traffic app that uses data from thousands of drivers to update traffic conditions in real time. Freelancers or gig workers complete a specific task or body of work, often known as deliverables, on a part-time or full-time, contractual basis.

A 2021 report by MBO Partners, an independent talent contracting firm, shared a surprising statistic. "The number of independent workers grew to over 51 million in 2021, an unprecedented 34% growth in a single year" (MBO Partners, 2021). The report explained some core reasons for the sharp increase: respondents referenced their need to supplement income, the scheduling flexibility that this arrangement brings, the inability to rely on full-time job security, and the digital tools available to make remote work more accessible (MBO Partners, 2021). These drivers are no surprise to anyone who managed daily life during the pandemic and is currently living with inflation.

Moreover, according to a 2019 CNBC report, "Freelancers doing skilled services earn a median rate of $28 an hour, earning more per hour than 70% of workers in the overall U.S. economy" (Booth, 2019). More than half of freelancers say, "No amount of money would entice them to take a traditional job" (Booth, 2019). The trend toward freelancing is not going away anytime soon. Educators tasked with preparing young people for careers must understand what gig work is and how it can be a viable and appealing option.

According to Edelman Intelligence, 90 million Americans will be freelancing by 2028. Does 90 million seem like a lot? It should; it constitutes the majority of the American workforce (Stahl, 2022). As you can imagine, hiring freelancers on an as-needed basis or even crowdsourcing work brings benefits to employers. By hiring talent this way, employers are only paying for the time needed to complete a project or task. They are not paying benefits or granting sick leave, and they can readily access a wide pool of individuals who are experts in a variety of discrete tasks. They do not need to find so many skills and capabilities in one person. According to *Forbes*, "Companies are increasingly thinking of work as project-based rather than role-based" (Lau, 2021). Of course, there are potential downsides like a lack of consistent team cohesion, company culture issues, missing institutional knowledge, and additional time needed for training, selecting, and onboarding each time a new project starts. Time will tell if the speculation around the volume of freelancers will come to fruition.

If the Future of Work is project-based, what does this mean for our students? To start, it means that following their passions and interests can still be a viable path if they can situate themselves successfully for project-based work. It means they can still win by being highly specialized in one area. It also means that they need a wide range of skills to find and maintain many clients and keep their finances in check without a singular, reliable paycheck from one employer.

Here are a few skills and mindsets students might need to develop over time to thrive as freelance, project-based, gig workers:

- Developing and maintaining the motivation to self-start when no one is setting a schedule for them.
- Working backwards from a deliverable to achieve a goal using backwards planning and execution skills.
- Knowing themselves and being able to reflect and capitalize on their strengths—for example, do they work best in the morning or evening, need to set a daily goal to get the work done over time, and so on.
- Time management skills—for example, planning mealtimes and breaks, self-care, taking meetings, responding to emails, and so on.
- Personal responsibility—for example, arriving to meetings on time, completing tasks, and so on.
- Client-facing communication skills.
- Money management and financial literacy—for example, in the United States, additional tax planning may be needed when working without a W-2 form.
- Knowledge of digital tools and digital literacy.

- Prospecting and sales skills—for example, finding new clients and closing the deal for each engagement.
- Customer experience skills—for example, building and maintaining a client base so that the same employers keep coming back.

It's easy to feel bogged down by isolating the specific skills when they are unsure of exactly what the job environment entails. One teacher recently said to me, without any hesitation, "I have been teaching for 25 years, and this is my only job. I do not have the first idea of what happens in other professions." In a future chapter, I will break down how we can examine an activity on-the-job and consider the skills necessary to complete that activity.

But as the preceding list highlights, it is possible to predict meaningful skills based on who, how, and where the work will get done—even without deep expertise in a particular role. The goal of this chapter is not to discretely cover and conquer each skill needed for the Future of Work, but instead to start to think about the implications of the Future of Work—to begin making connections to what's already happening within the classroom that will support students in being successful in these new ways of working.

Try to put yourself in the shoes of a worker and brainstorm with your students: "What do you think you will need to do in order to do a good job as a freelancer?" Their answers, and yours, may surprise you. Also, many schools have access to business partners and employment programs within the school that can lend support in this area.

Again, the concept of gig work or crowdsourcing may be unappealing to you or your learners. It might feel less stable and therefore less appropriate to pursue. It certainly feels different than how our own generation, or that of our parents, saw success at work. My father, for example, worked at the same company my entire life and often reveled in the sense of security and reliability that came from the steady work. He left every day at 8 a.m. and returned at 5:15 p.m. My own values were highly influenced by seeing him wake up every day, put on a suit, and commute to work. Given that the majority of the American workforce is expected to freelance by 2028, this reality is simply not available for most future employees.

By anchoring in this description of "a good job," we run the risk of turning our learners off to an increasingly viable way of working. It could lead us to respond negatively to a student if they say they want this job arrangement or a career in an industry known to hire talent this way. Knowing that it is becoming the norm can help us construct a more supportive response. We can even be the first to tell them that this is an upward trend in the world of work.

Knowing that freelancing is viable in the present and future can help us to reframe our thinking. The knowledge of the skills needed to be successful can help us integrate important elements into our teaching and highlight to students that what they are doing in the classroom will set them up for success on the job.

How the Work Is Done

SHRM categorized how work of the future is done into three categories:

- AI—this includes tasks normally accomplished by intelligent beings (namely, humans) being done by digital computers or other technologies.
- Robotics—this includes work accomplished by machines that has been traditionally completed by human beings. It includes the design, construction, and maintenance of the robots in question, both the hardware and software required.
- Automation—this includes the use of computers and machines to accomplish tasks once performed by human beings as well as tasks that were previously impossible based on human limitations.

Right away, the common thread running through these definitions is glaringly obvious: the replacement of tasks once done by human beings. Educator or not, you and everyone around you has encountered at least some of these technologies directly in your day-to-day life. Others may not be directly experienced, but you benefit from their existence less directly.

- Chatbots for customer service on websites.
- Meeting schedulers.
- Price forecasting tools that impact an item's final retail price.
- Inventory management software.
- Customer order-taking in restaurant, entertainment, or hospitality settings.

- Novel robots and cobots performing inspections, deliveries, and factory work for goods we use and purchase.
- Drug compounding robots mixing drugs in a pharmacy.
- Automotive robots performing a variety of tasks on assembly lines (painting, welding, counting, assembling, quality control).

Most students today have little memory of living life before automation and AI were integrated into daily life. Helping them reflect on the presence of this technology can lead them to greater curiosity about this most disruptive innovation. Consider reflection on the following questions, both on your own and with your learners.

- What kinds of tasks might AI complete that were previously performed by humans?
- What skills might I need in a workplace where AI is present?
- What aspects of a role or industry are beyond the influence that AI, robotics, and automation might have?

These forces that drive automation are not all bad. They can replace mundane tasks that many workers did not like doing and can improve productivity for employers. When the disruption of AI looms over any discussion about or preparation for the workplace, it is critically important to remind students of the need to be a lifelong learner. These changes are here and will continue to expand and impact how work gets done and our role in it. The human skills that our students will need, like being adaptable and open to being re-skilled, are evergreen and the best antidote to any anxieties around automation and AI disrupting their targeted industry.

Yes, it is easy to feel uncomfortable here—to feel as though the stability of the jobs market is weak and getting weaker. But these fears are not new. As early as the 16th century, but more popularized in the 19th and 20th century, some people have stoked fear that automation will cost us jobs—even as other voices have hailed automation as transformative for the workforce, wages, and labor market. The truth is, both sides are telling the truth.

I remember reading education articles in 2012 with titles such as "Will MOOCs replace the role of the teacher?" My colleagues and I felt nervous that teaching jobs could become obsolete. If you are not familiar, *MOOC* means "massive open online course" and popular examples such as Coursera, EdX, or Khan Academy are used widely in a variety of contexts. We quickly learned that independent online courses, while holding a specific value in select learning journeys, could not fully replace the noncognitive skills instruction as readily as some of the teaching components for the "hard" skills. Also, other important components that contribute to overall academic success, like mentorship and social supports, were essential to short-term and long-term impact—and unlikely to be accomplished with a set of log-in credentials to an otherwise successful MOOC.

While automation and robots in the workplace may have not come as fast as we might have imagined and have not replaced jobs in the way many predicted, they have had an impact. Importantly, and not surprisingly, the impact of this shift toward automation, robotic technology, and AI has been vastly different for different populations, geographic areas, and job sectors. So, it will impact our students at different rates.

For example, the automobile industry has been an early adopter of robots in the manufacturing of vehicles. Robots, as a specific example of technological automation, have a measurably negative effect on the labor market and wages. A 2020 study found that in 19 industries and 722 commuting zones, there was a "negative relationship between a commuting zone's exposure to robots and its post-1990 labor market outcomes" (Brown, 2020). In other words, robots have replaced jobs within the automobile industry in certain geographies.

In some ways, our worst fears are coming true. The study also noted that "adding one robot to an area reduces employment in that area by about six workers." With robots deployed at a rate of two to five per thousand workers in some of America's manufacturing and industrial zones—Kentucky, Louisiana, Missouri, Texas, Virginia, and Detroit, specifically—and with those rates expected to double or quadruple by 2025, the impact on the labor market, workforce, and wages will be significant.

But a closer look reveals something else: researchers differentiate between displacement effect and productivity effect. Displacement effect is about literally displacing jobs (see earlier), often for the benefit of industry and the business owners and stakeholders. A robot on the shop floor means fewer humans on the shop's payroll. But productivity effect reflects a more robust shift in the nature of work, allowing for easier job and task completion for existing human roles. This effect also captures the creation of new jobs and tasks that did not previously exist.

Yes, this level of automation continues to benefit industry, business owners, and stakeholders, but it also presents an opportunity to train, reskill, and upskill generations of learners for jobs that continue to emerge. We as educators and trainers can't influence whether a business or industry embraces productivity effect in equal proportion to displacement effect. But it's important to be comprehensive in our understanding of these forces.

That's not to bury the lead. Yes, robots are taking some of our jobs. Daron Acemoglu finds that, "In the U.S., especially in the industrial heartland, we find that the displacement effect is large (Brown, 2020)." Robots are replacing the jobs that we are often quite worried about—entry-level manufacturing and industrial jobs that pay decent wages and provide benefits without requiring advanced education or degrees. These are the jobs that have the potential to lead to careers and shift generational wealth, lifting families out of poverty. "When those jobs disappear," Acemoglu states, "those workers go and take other jobs from lower wage workers. It has a negative effect, and demand goes down for some of the retail jobs and other service jobs." In other words, changes toward robotics and automation impact more than the immediate business experiencing displacement effect.

The World Economic Forum (WEF) published its "The Future of Jobs Report 2023," drawing findings from a data set of over 673 million jobs. The report found that within the next five years, the global economy is expected to see job growth of 69 million jobs and a decline of 83 million jobs. This means a net decrease of 14 million jobs, or 2% of current employment ("The Future of Jobs 2023," April 2023). This hard reality requires educators to support students in new ways—by developing skills needed for success across multiple contexts and environments, by equipping them with the knowledge about the ever-changing workforce, and by fostering a thirst to be lifelong learners who can follow their passions and interests through continuous learning toward self-fulfillment.

All hope is not lost. Students can make themselves relevant, even in times of intense change. No man is an island; neither is any robot, computer program, or data set. Each technological asset is a part of a system designed to deliver an outcome. And the systems do still require humans. Specific software, hardware, robots, and data-driven AI tools are so far defined systems that meet a specific need or solve a specific problem. Companies invest in specific technology for specific purposes, and no one technological asset as, "The ability to adapt to entirely novel situations is still an enormous challenge for AI and robotics and a key reason why companies continue to rely on human workers for a variety of tasks. Humans still excel at social interaction, unpredictable physical skills, common sense, and, of course, general intelligence" (Brown, 2020). Educators can't train students to process data at the speed of light, but we can teach, practice, and assess the ability to interact with others, to respond to surprising circumstances, to apply good judgment, and to make good on baseline knowledge and skills.

The MIT researchers note that these systems are task-oriented and rarely would replace the full set of activities that make up a specific job. For an individual worker, this can result in a decrease in some tasks and an increase in time spent on other tasks—maybe even those they like better. In reporting for the Brookings Institution, a public policy research organization, Harry Holzer notes, "More broadly, workers who can complement the new automation, and perform tasks beyond the abilities of machines, often enjoy rising compensation. However, workers performing similar tasks, for whom the machines can substitute, are left worse off" (Holzer, 2022). As humans and technology have no choice but to coexist, the advantage is clear for job seekers who are more comfortable interacting with technical systems and processes.

To this end, consider in your own practice embracing a new focus—one that shifts classroom activities from mundane, transactional, or recall-based experiences to those that are authentic and promote critical thinking skills and decision-making. Instead of asking students to recall information or telling them something that they will regurgitate later, ask them to tackle a real-world task by using their judgment and a variety of other tasks to solve the problem. Ask them to brainstorm a solution to a problem that includes a wild, fantastical technological component—as well as the human side to bring that outlandish idea to life. In doing so, you'll be fostering many of the essential skills the WEF captured in its 2023 report, as noted in Figure 1.3.

Here, the beauty of education comes in, and educators shine. I have had the absolute privilege of hiring and observing countless teachers and have seen such incredible skill in providing problem-solving and critical-thinking prompts, all setting up students for success in their careers and their lives. In future chapters, we will dig into authentic problem solving as a classroom activity, including a Spotlight Story that shines a practical and encouraging light on the topic.

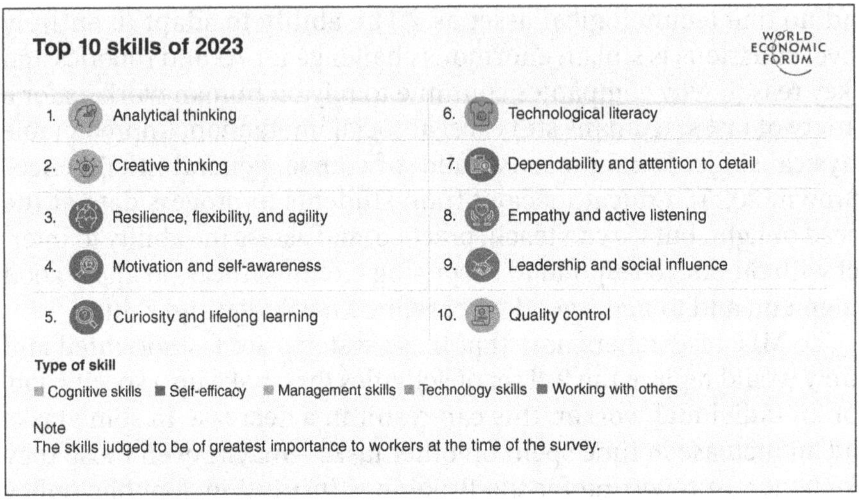

Top 10 skills of 2023
WORLD ECONOMIC FORUM
1. Analytical thinking
2. Creative thinking
3. Resilience, flexibility, and agility
4. Motivation and self-awareness
5. Curiosity and lifelong learning
6. Technological literacy
7. Dependability and attention to detail
8. Empathy and active listening
9. Leadership and social influence
10. Quality control
Type of skill
Cognitive skills
Self-efficacy
Management skills
Technology skills
Working with others
Note
The skills judged to be of greatest importance to workers at the time of the survey.

Figure 1.3: Top 10 skills of 2023.

Source: World Economic Forum.

FROM THE PERSONAL ARCHIVE

I've worked remotely for seven years and have experienced remote working benefits and drawbacks firsthand. Since the Future of Work involves remote work for more and more people, a peek behind the curtain of my working experience could prove helpful for those new to it.

At first, it was quite an adjustment period for me. I felt like every waking minute needed to be productive since I was not commuting to a workplace. This led to working long hours with few breaks. I had "work from home guilt" even though I put in even more hours and was meeting my employer's expectations. It turned unhealthy relatively quickly.

Through trial and error, and some deep reflection, I avoided the impending downward spiral of overwork that leads to burnout. I learned how to balance my workdays and build in breaks. The more I learned about myself in that new work environment, the better I could employ strategies to support myself.

At the end of the day, the lack of commute allows me to be present more with my family, and I appreciate the option to move to other parts of the country without losing my job if I so choose. But even with those perks, it wasn't a totally easy adjustment to make. I had well over a decade of work experience under my belt, and being in my thirties, I'd developed some self-awareness and reflection skills, and a regular yoga and meditation practice that helped me handle the highs and lows. Not everyone will be in the same situation or come to remote work with the same toolbox as me. It's important, then, that educators lay the foundation for healthy remote working practices for our students.

On the flip side, I have also supervised some people who have felt lonely in the remote work environment and had to create ways to feel more connected socially while working remotely. I share this experience to help others understand the realities of remote work and think about how we can support and guide students who might go this route. Of course, there are some roles where hybrid or remote work is not possible. For example, many healthcare roles and roles within the food and beverage industry cannot be done remotely. However, it is important to understand this trend and identify how our classrooms can lay the foundation for successful hybrid work.

Giving Students the Advantage

There are many opportunities for educators to structure student activities to mimic some of the workplace realities we covered in this chapter. Group projects, independent explorations, digesting asynchronous online materials—possibilities abound, and expert educators will find new ways to give learners autonomy and agency in the classroom. Yet doing so leaves a lot up to chance, and chance feels risky. After all, being prescriptive about where, when, and how the work gets done in a classroom or training setting is usually most efficient. Given that teachers never have enough time to get through everything they need to cover, efficiency is a top priority.

Yet, innovation is an iterative and vibrant process. It doesn't have to be perfect, and there will always be wins and losses when you try something new. The rest of *Shift Teaching Forward* aims to equip and inspire you to innovate with your students in relation to the knowledge, skills, and aptitudes they need to thrive at work. By bringing the

Future of Work into your classroom, even in small ways, you give your students an advantage—an advantage rooted in a frank, honest, and curious understanding of how their world is changing.

We want our students to develop a sense of personal responsibility for themselves. The world is changing, and they have the power to change along with it—with your help, if they choose. By exposing them to what's here and what's about to come, you're helping them look ahead with open eyes. And when it comes to enhancing employability, that's a great place to start.

Reflections and Intentions

- What are you doing in your classroom already that will help students thrive in the workplace environments described in this chapter?
- What are the job sectors that your students are interested in, and how might the elements described in this chapter impact those sectors? If you're not sure, how can you and your students find out together?
- What else will you do to continue to remain knowledgeable about the shifts coming with the Future of Work?

2 The Connection between Education and Employment

"We can't just go out and throw up some ads and hire some skilled people. The numbers just are not out there. High schools and colleges in the U.S. are not turning out graduates with the mix of technical expertise, soft skills, problem-solving ability, and communication skills that companies like Toyota need."

—Dennis Park, Assistant Manager of Toyota North American Production Support Center (Gaulden & Gottlieb, 2017)

The workplace is changing, and the Future of Work will bring new and unpredictable opportunities and challenges in the coming years. Educational institutions must show up for young people considering this truth, and that will require innovation. Teachers and trainers need to prepare students for a fulfilling career, whether the launch of that career is in a few years or a few weeks. Students and educators both face barriers to success, but by shifting our thinking and embracing new approaches, we can offer enduring and valuable experiences that will pay off on the job.

The goal of K–12 education cannot be to simply earn enough credits and commendations to get into a university or college. Nor can the goal of a training program be to simply get someone a certification that may or may not help them secure a new job. Education must now, more than ever, nurture the knowledge, skills, and aptitudes that support adaptability, a hunger to always learn, and an abiding sense of optimism about the world that lies ahead.

FROM THE PERSONAL ARCHIVE

I lived the automatic preference for and deference to collegiate education. For many, many years, it fueled a persistent belief that college was the best path to success for everyone.

Growing up, my family conditioned me and my siblings to believe that college was the absolute only path for a young person directly out of high school. At that time, I thought, "If you did not go to college, that is the end of your destiny." My mom didn't go to college (although the bookkeeping job she held straight out of high school would eventually be replaced by two people to keep up her same pace of work when she left!). While she really wanted to work from our home, I know she wanted differently for us. She wanted careers that would leave us able to independently sustain ourselves.

My father grew up with the same college focus. My father was a first-generation college graduate, a fortunate outcome that was not guaranteed. My grandfather, his father, desperately wanted to go to college and be a teacher. But life happened. He stayed at home to support his parents and sought work in a skilled trade.

Given his own missed opportunity, my grandfather always wanted his children to have all that college could offer. He started practicing welding for free until he was good enough to get paying work for the skill. Even though my grandfather became a successful welder and foreman at a ship-building company, he never lost sight of his dreams for his children. He provided for his family well in a modest and beautiful brick house he and my grandmother built by hand. He drove a company car and adorned our holiday tables with meats awarded to him for strong work.

Despite my grandfather's unrealized desire to attend college, he was still able to provide for his family without a college degree. Somehow the power of that truth didn't sound as loudly in our family as the importance of going to college, at least when I was a young child.

When I worked at an urban charter school, I felt the same pressure to focus on college. This time, however, I was part of the machine maintaining the belief in our school and surrounding community that college was king. Everything we focused on scaffolded toward college preparations—excelling on standardized tests, reading certain texts, endless discussions about different colleges and universities to which our students would one day apply.

We didn't spend a lot of time—any, if I'm frank—talking about other types of excellence or different ways to envision life past high school. If you wanted a career, then you went to college. The students I supported in elementary school are now long out of high school. I think of them often and hope they found their way to careers that sustain their lives and ignite their passions—through college, training, or any other pathway that was right for them. I hope with all I've got that they found a way to personal fulfillment, inspiration, and satisfying careers that meet their personal and professional goals.

Given I have worked as an educator across so many different settings, I can confidently say that the lesson here is that there is not one path that works for everyone. We have to hold the many truths at once and be open to zigzags and wrong turns along the journey to personal and professional fulfillment. A university degree might be a "right now," "maybe later," or "not in this lifetime," and it depends on a variety of factors. However, exposing students to careers and teaching employability skills are a good idea all of the time, regardless of the immediate next step in a student's learning journey.

The Bridge between Secondary Education and Employment

I began working in the workforce development sector in 2016. This is a crowded and necessary space in the United States, with several entities all contributing to training and skilling people for job opportunities. Vocational schools, nonprofit organizations, government workforce boards, for-profit training institutions, career coaches—there's a nearly endless list of people, organizations, and companies contributing to the work of getting people working.

Despite the myriad players at the table, I learned very quickly that there weren't many comprehensive solutions getting scalable success. More often, there were isolated or small-scale successes only focusing on narrow solutions. McKinsey & Company is a global management consulting firm that routinely conducts deep research to help bring visibility and solutions to complex challenges. In 2012, the company released "Education to Employment: Designing a System that Works"—a report based, in part, on survey data from 8,000 educators, students, and employers. It covered the challenges young people faced in securing meaningful employment as well as those faced by employers seeking to find suitable talent. The report indicated that there was a "heterogeneous and fragmented nature of job-training systems" and that while "multiple entities are involved . . . responsibility typically is shared among education, labor and industry departments" and that "no-one has a birds-eye view of the whole process" (McKinsey & Company, 2012). Across the globe, training efforts focus on discrete aspects of career success. No one entity was able to guide a learner from A to Z, and tremendously talented people kept slipping through the cracks.

Currently, I am the Chief of Learning at Generation, a global nonprofit workforce development organization that was founded in part because of that 2012 report. My team supports the design, implementation, and evaluation of training programs in several countries around the world. Generation aims to provide a comprehensive solution all along the education to employment journey from securing job vacancies from the start, deeply understanding the job role and employer needs, training that includes integrated skills, and supporting students with social supports and mentorship. My work at Generation has informed my view on the connection between education and employment. The hunger to share what I've learned, coupled with my varied experiences in education, fueled the writing of this book.

We know that closing the gap between education and employment has not been consistently accomplished across the globe. With the global unemployment rate hovering around 6%, hundreds of millions of people who want to work are unable to secure employment. Educators are already doing important and remarkable work empowering students and fostering their success, but we also know that we still have a need for more equitable and effective educational practices that provide students a bridge to successful careers.

Given the common disconnection between secondary schools and employment opportunities, it's easy to see how young people might miss the chance to learn about the world of work, the types of careers that are growing in demand, and the way the Future of Work is shifting. If the mission of a high school is to prepare learners for college, and most higher education institutions prepare learners for "a well-rounded higher education for a lifetime of meaning and service"

(Wolff & Booth, 2017), then employability is not always an explicit priority. It seems like exploring a career is the "side job" of students and of most institutions. There might be separate career programs or centers where students can proactively receive their services or be lucky enough for someone to give them an opportunity to explore various career pathways and learn employability skills. For those who went on to college immediately after high school, where along their journey did they have an opportunity to significantly explore their career options and increase their employability skills? Misconceptions about both the value proposition of college and the requirements needed for a career can negatively impact students. Our goal should be to equip them with the knowledge, skills, and abilities needed to follow their interests and lead to personal fulfillment.

Regardless of a student's immediate experience after their time with you in the classroom, having the following in their toolkit will give them an advantage:

- Knowledge of what the workplace is like and how to succeed there.
- Experiences and explorations that let them test their interests and "try on" different professions from a variety of fields.
- Instruction and abundant practice in applying universal skills that are ever so important in the workplace.

The more authentic the environment in which to have acquired the preceding, the better poised for success the learner will be.

Both teachers and learners are negatively impacted by the stigma against "job training" or "vocational training" that has not been as publicly favored as college preparatory programs. Historically, many students who may not have performed at high levels according to report cards and standardized tests were pushed to more vocational routes that accepted lower grade point averages. This may sound antiquated—like something that was true in the 20th century but no longer a widely held practice. Alas, that is not so. "A Snapshot of Vocational Education" by the Student Research Foundation and data from Brookings states that, "The number of CTE (Career and Technical Education) credits earned by US High School students declined 14% between 1990 and 2009, in large part because high schools were ramping up their focus on preparing students for college" (Kamarck, 2022).

This is not because vocational training offerings are lagging in response to market shifts. In 1992, popular course categories included "agriculture, health, marketing and distribution, trade and industry, and technical and communications," compared to 2018 when offerings included "AI, App development, computer graphics, cybersecurity, forensics, pre-engineering and robotics" (Student Research Foundation, 2018). It seems that the vocational and technical training courses themselves have shifted with the times; however, our perception of them has not.

Today, the training landscape has arisen to fill a gap left by the colleage-focused secondary school system. Many different training programs target learners of all kinds with different price points, formats, and content covered. Some are training for training's sake, solely focusing on technical skills and certifications without a focus on job placement or employability skills for graduates. Some technical programs do work with employers to secure internship or employment vacancies by the end of the program; other have dedicated time in the program spent preparing learners to apply for roles and shine in interviews. Both online and in-person tech boot camps abound, ready to train in technical skills needed in computer programming, cloud computing, database management software development, and more. There are massive open online courses (MOOCs) where learners can gain skills and certifications (that may or may not improve employability). These can be taken to supplement existing educational experiences or college coursework. Employers themselves offer skilling courses, both related to the job at hand or offered to empower existing employees to grow into new roles. For-profit colleges also abound, offering role-based certifications and degrees (often at a tremendous cost).

The sheer number of career-training options available for job seekers suggested that the ever-changing future has not typically been a focus for K–12 school systems. Between the options of letting things remain the same and embracing a total redesign of American high schools, there is a lot of space to experiment with giving employability its due. Our young people face barriers to a more equitable future if we don't.

My own experiences and research for this book came from a variety of educational contexts: K–12, university, and nonprofit job-training programs. Outside of job-training programs, where the explicit goal is job readiness and immediate entry into a career, I have not seen employability skills integrated into the day-to-day experience for students at scale. Excellent outliers exist, and some are featured in these pages. There may be specific job-readiness programs that occur separate from the classroom; however, it is common that the social-emotional and career-readiness skills are not typically integrated into the classroom setting with an eye toward employability. One educator I interviewed noted, "It feels almost cold, being focused like that on jobs. Isn't school about becoming the best human you can be? Not just trying to get a job?"

I understand the tension. No one wants to reduce learners down to their ability to earn income-neither in a high school setting nor in a jobs-training program where that is, in fact, the focus of the experience. But pretending that employment isn't an essential component of adulthood is unfair and limiting. As with many things in life, leaning into one extreme or another doesn't provide real solutions. If we are happy with saying that employability is only the concern of post-secondary options, what does that mean for the millions of learners who do not attend a college or university after graduating high school? They deserve to thrive in adulthood as much as college graduates do. Vocational training could be one answer, but many students are enrolled in districts that don't offer this experience.

If you find yourself struggling with positioning employability against the rest of your intended course content, sit with that feeling—don't ignore it. Ask yourself why this feels like it does, and what can you do to explore and mitigate that feeling. It is part of the educator's role to be a facilitator and cheerleader along a learner's journey and do what's possible, within our power, to set them up for success in this ever-changing world.

Challenges and Barriers

Success means something different for everyone. It's about how we meet the individual goals we set out for ourselves that leads to personal fulfillment. Because personal goals and fulfillment are unique to each of us, our definition of *good job* and *career success* are unique as well. Helping students begin to define their own view of career success will give them a north star to pursue as they grow and evolve. Consider the following list and whether your learners would benefit from exploring these criteria—abstractly in a future-based, vision-setting way, or concretely—as they seek a particular role in the near future.

Potential Job Outcomes, in No Particular Order

- Daily joy that stems from the work done, the people you work with, or the impact the work has.
- Being able to make your own choices on the path to and within a role.
- Alignment with your pre-existing expectations.
- Equitable and dignified treatment of you and peers in the workplace.
- A feeling of excitement and motivation at the beginning of a workday.
- Appropriate and fair compensation, including benefits.
- Flexibility in terms of when and where work takes place.
- A realistic and reliable path to promotion.
- The ability to work with others to achieve goals.
- Pathways for ongoing learning and development.
- Supportive management.

Learners will surely find other factors they'd like to add to the list, and prioritizing these items is sure to be a fun challenge. That said, if those are the successes that we are aiming for, we know that there are challenges learners face that hold them back from these happy outcomes. Some challenges I've seen myself, as well as others uncovered while writing this book. They include but are not limited to the following as shown in Figure 2.1.

To begin unpacking challenges faced by students and teachers, consider the experience of peers who have worked through similar circumstances.

Sage on the Stage, Guide on the Side

A former colleague of mine, Gideon Murenga, now works as a regional coordinator for a technical and vocational education training (TVET) for the German Society for International Cooperation in Nairobi, Kenya. On behalf of the German government, the organization, has been operating in Nairobi since 1975 to support vocational educational training

Students' Barriers to Employability	Teachers' Barriers to Integrating Employability Content
■ Placement in a binary path, college or career, instead of a lifelong learning pathway ■ A labor market powered by nepotism and casual favors that too often does not cross racial or economic lines ■ Lack of social capital that leaves internships and other real-work experiences being offered to only a select few ■ Lack of critical employability skills that are essential in the workforce, including both hard skills (e.g., digital literacy) and soft skills (e.g., communication, personal responsibility) ■ Feeling overwhelmed by choices, which can lead to inaction or having family/other influencers select a choice for them ■ Insufficient opportunities to explore and develop their passions and purpose	■ Pressure to "cover" standards and content, leaving no time for career path exploration and real-world learning opportunities ■ Not being trained to teach employability skills ■ Limited exposure to careers and career pathways available to students ■ Lack of connections with employers in the community ■ Disproportionate emphasis on standardized tests that incentivizes "Teaching to the Test"

Figure 2.1: Student and teacher barriers regarding employability.

for youth and adults. A key focus of Gideon's work has been supporting educators—"trainers" as they are referred to within his organization. He identified that bringing real-world experiences, references, and perspectives has been a challenge. Innovating on more traditional approaches to teaching to prepare students for the world they will enter has been a challenge as well.

He decided to work on a shift that moved past the traditional dynamic common in his classrooms: trainers were the owners of information, and students were the passive recipients of the knowledge. This is not aligned with the dynamic, collaborative, and ever-changing world that they will enter wherein employees will need to seek out their own answers and solutions to common problems.

Gideon started by working on a course that focused on the automotive industry. He and his trainers agreed that their students were entering class having already studied how a car engine works through real-world videos on YouTube. They wanted to leverage what they already know, so there was no need for instructors to be the center of knowledge. He noted that teachers can "grow what a student knows and is passionate about" and have the power to ignite the flame. He and his team sought to recreate learning experiences that featured different inroads to projects, allowing learnings to work in existing knowledge that was meaningful to them.

In doing so, Gideon was moving his trainers away from the traditional "Sage on the Stage" model for teaching. This model holds the instructor as the center of all knowledge and evaluation in a classroom. Educators who are used to that approach may feel apprehension if asked to hand off the baton, or support classroom activities involving content in which they aren't expert. Consider the educator who shared that she had no idea what other careers were like; moving away from Sage on the Stage while integrating employability content can feel particularly uncomfortable. The professional development involved in supporting this model involves coaching, feedback, and modeling how to personalize learning based on activating prior knowledge—and using modern tools, like YouTube in this instance, that are available to students for exploring their passions and adding to their own learning.

A way to stoke the fires of interest in students is to embrace project-based experiences. By facilitating group collaboration to promote the critical thinking and analytical skills, we are moving the Sage on the Stage to the position of Guide on the Side. A Guide on the Side makes no presumption that they'll be able to answer all student questions—in fact, they make it clear that they shouldn't be expected to do this. This teacher creates flexible, open-ended projects with clear and rigorous criteria for success, and then takes a supportive position, guiding learners as they work through problems, answer research questions, and synthesize their discoveries.

These two little rhymes have long been a popular pair for juxtaposing two differing styles of teaching. For educators keen to increase employability, Guide on the Side is the way to go. As noted in Chapter 1, no one educator could ever stay abreast of the innumerous ways specific roles, jobs, or industries are changing in the face of digitization, automation, and AI. Embrace the uncertainty and support your learners as they seek answers for themselves.

Teachers who embody Guide on the Side have the most success when they commit to leaning into change and the discomforts associated with a new teaching model. Some beliefs that underpin this approach are:

- Teachers are lifelong learners.
- Some traditional ways of teaching are not serving the modern learner well.
- Teachers do not need to be the owners of knowledge.
- Learners have rich experiences they can bring into the classroom.

For some trainers and educators, this shift is natural. It's possible they never took on the role of Sage on the Stage and have always positioned themselves as facilitators and guides. For others, it involves a massive mindset shift that reorients them completely away from what they know well. This parallels the mindset shift needed to bring employability and the Future of Work into more secondary classrooms in general.

Of course, shifting to a learner-centered classroom where students have more power over what they learn and how is not an easy undertaking. Adding in the complexities of the Future of Work can exacerbate this. I spoke with dozens of teachers and trainers to gather perspectives for this chapter. Their insights confirm my own observations from across my career.

- Students may have a different risk tolerance when they imagine themselves working as adults. They may shy from any exploration of gig work or entrepreneurship as they've always imagined themselves in a "steady" full-time job. This could limit their perceived future options, given that the majority of U.S. workers are expected to be freelance by 2028, as noted in Chapter 1.
- Encouraging healthy risks and celebrating failure is an important aspect of learning, but not all classrooms are ready for this. When teachers model risk-taking and bring in stories and examples that highlight the upsides of risks, learners can feel more secure in thinking more broadly and experimentally about future careers.
- Students can add real value—not just in the future, but here and now as well. One teacher shared how she once brought local

community and business leaders into the classroom for career talks, expecting the benefit to be purely for the learners. The question-and-answer time exceeded everyone's expectations when the learners started sharing ideas and solutions back with the leaders. Everyone felt enriched by the experience.

- Young people can make their own decisions. Despite benefiting from inputs and advice from respected adults and family members, they are more capable than we sometimes acknowledge when it comes to career planning. This is especially true if the wisdom coming to them is some version of the adage, "Your career choices are doctor, lawyer, or failure."

Further chapters in this book will dive deeper into how to bring employability into your classroom. Here, it's important to situate ourselves in the persona shift needed to embrace the change.

Evolving Mindsets

Whether employability is an explicit goal of any school district, training program, or general context for education, the individual educator has the power to make important decisions. Deciding to prioritize your learners' future (and current) employability doesn't have to depend on a district mandate or school-funded program. Every classroom has the potential to embed dreaming, researching, and planning for work—as long as the educator driving the experience wills it to be so.

This prospect might seem daunting, or perhaps you've already been thinking about this as you've flipped through the pages of this book. In either case, your mindset around what is possible and why it is important will be a difference maker for whatever comes next.

Mindsets are complicated things. They develop over time and are based on millions and millions of experiences. They are influenced by our deepest values and beliefs—cultural, spiritual, and political. And they are notoriously stubborn and resistant to change. Yet if mindsets influence our interpretations of and responses to situations, then we better tune in to them and ask ourselves if those mindsets are truly productive in a learning environment.

The mindset of the educator in the classroom is so very important because students are sharp observers of things unsaid. They readily pick up on and interpret the mindset of the teacher based on myriad cues—verbal and nonverbal—that instructors send. Muenks et. al. (2020) conducted a longitudinal study of over 150 university STEM professors and thousands of students. They found that "students' perceptions of professors' mindsets can serve as a situational cue that affects students' motivation, engagement, and performance." This has both immediate and long-term effects. If you believe employability is worthy of time and consideration in your class, learners will know. If you don't, they'll know that, too.

Productive mindsets will help you, the educator, embrace the complexities and unknowns surrounding the Future of Work as well as how to bring it to your learners. Consider the productive mindsets and practices in Figure 2.2. Which resonate deeply, and which inspire you to think differently?

"If we could change ourselves, the tendencies in the world would also change." These are the words of Gandhi that often get restated as, "Be the change you wish to see in the world." The difference is subtle but significant. For educators, one of the most transformational moments comes in recognizing that your students' mindsets and learning behaviors reflect your own mindsets and learning behaviors. A leading thinker on growth mindset, Carol Dweck, defines growth mindset as a belief that intelligence is malleable and improvable. Learners who hold a growth mindset most often keep motivated by their own desire to learn, grow, and overcome challenges. For those learners who arrive at your doorstep without a deeply seated belief that they can grow and improve, your inherent belief on their behalf can make all the difference. We must go beyond accepting that challenges, mistakes, and failure are an unavoidable downside to the learning process. A growth mindset enables educators and their students to believe that mistakes and failure are essential and welcomed. Uncertainty, then, becomes a desirable state of being for the purposes of learning. What a wonderful way to approach preparing for the Future of Work.

The Importance of Equity in Education

It is essential for educators to do the work of inclusive and equitable teaching so that we are not, intentionally or otherwise, gatekeeping opportunity for women, students of color, and other groups who have

Mindset or Practice	Personal Beliefs	Application of Beliefs to Employability for Learners
Growth Mindset	Intelligence is not fixed; I can get better at things.	My students have what it takes to grow, evolve, and thrive in the unknown Future of Work. They are not limited by their current abilities.
Inquiry Learning	Learning is not a transaction. Learning is observing, describing, posing questions, exploring ideas, and practicing skills in context.	My students can achieve more when I allow them to pursue learning actively. Integrating new ways for them to accomplish work will help them become lifelong learners, thus helping them as they approach unknown careers.
Social and Public Learning	We most often learn together, and rarely learn alone. Sharing ideas and questions is key to self and others' learning.	My students need to work together and develop collaboration and communication skills. Those skills will empower them to thrive in multiple employment settings.
Metacognition and Reflection	I am empowered to think about my own thinking, my own self, my own struggles/obstacles, and my own learning.	My students should be similarly empowered. They will have many decisions to make as they develop their careers, and these skills will serve them well.
Feedback Mindset	I can ask for and receive feedback from others; I can offer constructive feedback when appropriate.	My students will get lots of feedback from co-workers, managers, and other stakeholders regardless of the career they choose. By facilitating these experiences now, I am setting them up to thrive later.
Self-Efficacy and Agency	I can make choices that positively impact my learning, career, and life path.	My students can do this, too. By giving them tools to support explorations and investigations, and by exposing them to what's possible, I support them as they guide their own journey.

Figure 2.2: Productive mindsets and practices.

been systemically left out of certain roles, pathways, and industries. If it were as easy as naming it and inspiring others to do it, we'd all be in a better place, enjoying the richness that fully equitable education and employment ecosystems would offer all of society. While breaking down systemic racism, sexism, and other systems that work against equity is far beyond the scope of this book, I could not leave this unsaid.

Early in my career, I received professional training around unconscious bias and equitable teaching practices. While I continue learning and am not perfect, I must use any platform I have to encourage equitable teaching and equal opportunity access to all. I choose to repeatedly do the learning and the work of supporting anti-racist and inclusive education.

The opportunity gap is staggering. Working hard is not enough to ensure the life one dreams of. Systemic barriers reinforce myths and stereotypes that maintain the status quo. We see all around us how systems and institutions continue to cause roadblocks. You have the power to learn how and then recognize when biases are influencing your actions, reflect on your own assumptions, and increase opportunities for your students.

SPOTLIGHT STORY: DE MONTFORT UNIVERSITY

De Montfort University (DMU) is a progressive higher education institution in Leicester, United Kingdom. DMU was named the best university in the U.K. for helping students build their careers in the National Undergraduate Employability Awards (2021). A defining feature of DMU is that many of its students are nontraditional. In this regard, many students are the first generation in their families to attend university and are typically drawn from low socio-economic backgrounds. DMU students are also highly diverse in terms of ethnicity and the proportion of students with disabilities. Given this diverse student population, inclusivity lies at the heart of DMU, and thanks to their remarkable career commitment, students are given incredible access to career support to allow them to compete against more traditional, privileged students.

Employability is fully integrated across DMU's educational ecosystem. Their program, DMU Works, is 100% dedicated to career success. Employability is also fully embedded within the curriculum. Three defining features struck me while investigating DMU's approach to employability: its proactive approach to nurturing a sense of belonging, its firm recognition that employability should be fully embedded within the curriculum in highly innovative ways, and its guarantee of securing work experience opportunities for all students.

We'll take a deeper dive into DMU's work in Chapter 6.

A Sense of Belonging

We are all familiar with campus fliers and promotions. Students are constantly exposed to various promotions to entice participation in wide-ranging career activities, from workshops and CV development activities to career fairs. However, what if you're a student who doesn't identify with careers outside of your historical exposure? For instance, if you have never heard of a particular role or position, there's a high chance that you, even at university, may not realize that this is a job you could ever attain. This is precisely what DMU Works discovered—it's not enough to just invite students to take up career-building opportunities.

This discovery led DMU Works first to identify the U.K. postcodes that were measurably disadvantaged and then identify its students who came from these areas. With a targeted email list, DMU Works invited identified students to participate in a career-building program. Despite this targeted approach, recruitment rates remained dismally low. Eager to help, the DMU Works team picked up the phone and personally reached out to each identified student. It turned out the students had seen the emails featuring images of office buildings but hadn't believed the opportunity was for them. In these highly compassionate telephone calls, the DMU Works team explained the predicament that many students, just like them, had in competing successfully against students with more resources, for example, personal networks—they too deserved a leg up in their careers.

With this proactive approach, recruitment picked up. Several students are now on a personalized program of specialist support to give them the employability boost they deserve. This example shows how important it is to be persistent and recognize that traditional promotion often isn't enough. Instead, we need to create a sense of belonging and identity to enable all students to realize how to take the best step forward to help their careers and fulfill their potential.

Embedding Employability into the Curriculum

Mastering subject matter has long been the core focus of education. Universities are no different. A typical university degree curriculum usually focuses on building specialist knowledge. Increasingly, universities and colleges realize they need to embed employability directly into the curriculum. It is not a nice-to-have add-on. DMU believes that a degree must incorporate employability into its learning objectives and, hence, class activities and assessment.

Across DMU's degree programs, the academic staff has done a fantastic job embedding real-world activities into the curricula. For example, DMU's Leicester Castle Business School embeds specialist class modules that focus on employability. Instead of a research dissertation, students can opt for a Business Research Project. In this instance, students work with local businesses and conduct research. This not only gives students the research experience they would normally get through writing a dissertation, but it is also business-facing. Importantly, they deal with real-world business problems and are given the opportunity to offer valuable insights that also help the local community.

Guaranteed Work Experience

In highly competitive graduate markets, having prior work experience is a résumé/CV must. This is relatively easy if you have access to social and family networks. This is not the case with many students from disadvantaged backgrounds. This is where DMU's work experience guarantee is so important. It provides students with the guaranteed option for early work experience to increase their chances of securing a high-profile placement—and DMU does place students with well-known companies like IBM and Bosch. A great initiative DMU offers is its Frontrunners program. This work experience program provides local businesses and academics incentives to hire students. Students are paid a living wage and gain precious experience while studying in their second year at the university.

For example, Fashion Purpose was an entrepreneurial initiative undertaken by two DMU educators. Over a couple of years, they recruited students from different subject areas (e.g., business, fashion, and computer science) to undertake specific job roles (e.g., social media marketing, app development, and fashion promotion). DMU Works also supported the process from start to finish. As students had to apply for the roles under competitive conditions, they were provided with plenty of advice and support to get the roles. Once hired, they undertook genuine teamwork and were expected to deliver several outcomes over nine months, the duration of the paid internship. In other words, DMU students gained real-world experience on campus that helped with student living costs and essential employability skills.

All told, DMU exemplifies how to boost employability among disadvantaged students. To make employability inclusive, however, we need to take a proactive, personalized approach, and embed and integrate employability across the whole university experience to help all students reach their potential.

Reflections and Intentions

- Of the educational contexts described, which resonates most with the one you are connected to?
- What are the specific barriers faced by teachers and students within your context?
- How do you describe your role in the education to employment continuum?
- What mindsets resonated with you? Which gave you pause?
- What ideas have been sparked from the DMU Spotlight Story that can be applied to your context?

3 Two Frameworks for Understanding Social-Emotional Skills

> *"Employer surveys consistently reveal that more than disciplinary knowledge and skills is needed to be successful in today's workplace—regardless of the field, level of education and level of work. What have traditionally been called 'soft skills' have in fact become essential employability qualities."*
>
> —*Wolff & Booth, 2017*

People skills. Critical thinking skills. Soft skills. Social-emotional learning. Durable skills. Behavioral skills. Aptitudes and attitudes. 21st-century skills.

Anyone who's spent even a few minutes in an educational setting in the last few decades has almost certainly heard at least one of those terms. From the youngest preschoolers to the most accomplished graduate student, many learners across the educational spectrum have been working through content under this umbrella.

No one would argue that these skills, whatever you call them, aren't important—in general education as well as in preparation for the world of work. There are, however, many ways to interpret and prioritize these skills, and infinite approaches for delivering the content and integrating it into new or existing trainings, courses, and programs. For the purposes of this book, we will refer to these skills as social-emotional skills, or Social-Emotional Learning (SEL).

SEL in the Jobs-Training Landscape

Historically, many vocational training programs focused on skills necessary to perform specific job tasks. The course syllabus or program contents focused on the tactical skills required—think teaching the steps to securely weld a 90-degree joint or how to rev up a machine at the beginning of a shift. Excellent teachers would work SEL into the learner experience, but on paper, there was rarely a clear focus on the softer aspects of the job—skills like working collaboratively in a team, responding to feedback from a supervisor, or managing one's stress under the pressure of meeting timelines.

This is still evidenced today; most recently, I saw a course syllabus for a state-governed program for a Certified Nursing Assistant (CNA) program. Anyone familiar with the work of a CNA knows that patience, grace under pressure, and the ability to do unpleasant physical tasks without giving up are table stakes for success on the job. However, these skills are not covered on the course scope and sequence. The state governing body, however, needed to ensure with the utmost fidelity that programs training CNAs were uniform and objective across the state. This meant that zero modifications or additions to the course syllabus could be entertained—even if it meant better preparing graduates for the challenges they would certainly face once on the job.

On the other side of the coin, some career readiness programs focus on SEL and employability skills like Self-Awareness, Relationship Skills, or preparing a résumé without explicit connections to an industry or role. This is understandable given the additional research, time and specificity that it takes to create profession-specific employability content can be a barrier. However, these nuances are essential to ensure relevant application. The expectation is that by arming job hunters with SEL and employability skills, they'll be better positioned in the marketplace regardless of the career they are targeting.

The ideal shift is to teach technical skills and social-emotional skills in an integrated way. In doing so, learners will see the connection between the two sets of skills and understand the value both add to their desirability as a future teammate. "Demonstrating required skills" means more when the required skills combine hard and soft skills through authentic practice and application.

This is not easily done. For some roles, it's easier to blend and practice these skill sets in an instructional setting. Consider the work of an insurance salesperson. Soft skills like reading people's body language, handling rejection, managing your own time, and attentively listening readily integrate with the hard skills of presenting a product's value proposition and delivering a compelling close to lock in a sale. Then consider the work of a computer programmer. Teamwork, asking for help, managing time, and building your confidence are critically important, but hard to simulate in a practice environment that requires working on a lab for two hours independently.

These challenges should energize instructors and curriculum designers, not scare them away. When we integrate soft and hard skills together, we amplify the impact of both for our learners.

FROM THE PERSONAL ARCHIVE

Through my work at Generation, I have been fortunate enough to travel the world and shadow individuals performing jobs across four industry sectors: healthcare, customer service, technology, and manufacturing. Regardless of the country or the sector, there were common reasons why individuals were unsuccessful on the job. Time and again, supervisors and human resources leads would say, "It's not a lack of technical knowledge that forced us to let someone go." Instead, they'd describe how employees lacked the social-emotional skills necessary for success in their company.

Three reasons were cited by supervisors repeatedly—across industry sectors and across borders: attendance and punctuality, communication, and attitude. So rarely would we hear about a reprimand or termination based on being unable to do the technical work. Yet, I heard tale after tale about teammates who were terminated because they repeatedly did not arrive on time and could not maintain professional relationships with peers and supervisors. When I interviewed high performers in the role, they would describe past colleagues in similar terms. "'So and so' was really good at the work, but they just couldn't get along with anyone."

I remember meeting Derek, a construction helper from Texas. The role of a construction helper is to be on the spot and able to help the more senior tradespeople and construction workers on a residential or commercial build site. It was a great role with incredible growth potential as it was a reliable entry point to a highly skilled trade such as pipefitting, welding, or carpentry.

Derek was struggling to arrive at work on time. He explained to me that that day, he woke up in plenty of time to arrive to work. However, his car did not start. He didn't have another option, and by the time he waited for the next bus, he knew he would be late. He chose to not call his supervisor and proceeded to not show up to work the following three days; this designated him as a "no show/no call" and meant three days without pay.

As I spent more time with him, I learned that Derek did not call his supervisor because he had never done that before and wasn't sure how to even start the conversation. A crippling combination of lack of exposure, fear, lack of adaptive communication skills, and poor decision-making led to a web that was difficult to untangle. When I left his build site that day, he felt uncertain whether he'd be able to stick it out or not in this field.

To close the gap between what students can offer and what employers demand, we need to teach SEL and employability skills. Outside employment outcomes, SEL learning equips people with the skills we want to see in our friends, partners, neighbors. We want to send young people into the world fully able to make sound decisions, be courageous in the face of challenges, and use critical thinking in daily life. Of course, employers want the exact same abilities in their workforce.

I've come to believe that the following truths are undeniable and of the utmost importance for any educator or trainer who hopes to improve employment outcomes for their learners:

- Social-emotional skills are crucial to success in the workplace; as teachers, we need to understand what skills employers are looking for learners to demonstrate.
- There is no "one-size-fits-all" approach to teaching social-emotional skills; we perform our teaching role better when we adapt to learner needs.
- We need to get real; our teaching must be grounded in on-the-job realities.

- As teachers, we can facilitate, model, and enable successful competency-building along the student employability journey.

Social and emotional competencies are a top priority for employers. Therefore, educators must teach content that supports those competencies to connect employability and on-the-job realities. If not us, who? If we accept this challenge, we can help our students succeed in the workplace while also helping employers secure talent they need. You may be in a context where your students are entering the workforce right away or where the next step is college or university. Maybe your learners are considering military service. Regardless of where they are in their journey, the benefits of introducing, integrating, and practicing technical skills, SEL, and employability will sow seeds of success in their life and future career.

Our ability to attend to technical skills is limited to the context of our teaching. And as covered in Chapter 1, the world of work is changing so quickly that even highly focused role-based training programs can't predict the actual skills needed soon. And many educators teach content that quite simply does not connect to future careers. The call to action is clear, even if an educator's path forward feels challenging. If teaching technical skills is not possible given your context, endeavor to focus on and support activities, sessions, and experiences that increase a learner's SEL and employability skills.

What Is Social and Emotional Learning?

Before SEL can be integrated into any curriculum, the educator facilitating it needs to know what constitutes social and emotional learning. A universal definition of SEL doesn't exist, but the definition shared by the Collaborative for Academic, Social, and Emotional Learning (CASEL) resonates most with me. CASEL is a multidisciplinary network made up of researchers, educators, practitioners, and child advocates across the United States. It exists to support programming, research, legislation, and implementation of evidence-based social-emotional learning. CASEL defines SEL as follows:

> *SEL is the process through which all young people and adults acquire and apply the knowledge, skills, and attitudes to*

develop healthy identities, manage emotions and achieve personal and collective goals, feel, and show empathy for others, establish, and maintain supportive relationships, and make responsible and caring decisions.

Three key factors stand out in this definition. SEL is . . .

- **A process**—an ongoing, living, evolving journey. The process is a journey that everyone is continuously on, including educators.
- **Multifaceted**—SEL includes several aspects of learning: knowledge, skills, and attitudes.
  - Knowledge—information that you can name and and repeat, even without necessarily applying it, for example, "What is teamwork?"
  - Skills—abilities that achieve certain outcomes, for example, describing and demonstrating how to be an excellent team player.
  - Attitudes—feelings and mindsets that influence your ways of being, for example, "I want to be a great team player, and I'll do whatever it takes."
- **Outcome-driven**—SEL aims to achieve several outcomes:
  - Developing a sense of self-identity.
  - Managing emotions.
  - Achieving goals for students and their communities.

It also extends to social relationships and speaks of personal responsibility, caring for others, and effective decision-making. When done well, students own their learning and continual growth of these skills as a self-managed process over time.

SEL has the power to be ambitious and transformative. Its flexibility is a big part of the reason why. Direct instruction of SEL can occur at any level. Educators can direct SEL toward a specific student of any age level, a classroom, or an entire institution. It can thrive in secondary schools, colleges, universities, and vocational training centers. You can teach specific social awareness skills to one class or roll out a district wide SEL program.

Regardless of how it is delivered, one universal belief drives all SEL activities—the belief that social and emotional knowledge, skills, and attitudes are nameable, teachable, and learnable. This point cannot be emphasized enough. If an educator thinks SEL is unknowable and untouchable, their ability to impart it to their learners is severely hampered. Consider what was covered in Chapter 2 around the educator's mindset. Too many students, and teachers, wrongly believe that social and emotional skills are fixed or preset. Yet my own experiences and my research both tell a different story. Social and emotional competencies are not set personality traits. Anyone can learn these skills and doing so is crucial for success.

Which SEL Skills Need to Be Taught?

For educators and trainers new to SEL, knowing where to start can be daunting—even more so if your district or organization is not implementing a program or curriculum across the board. There are so many frameworks and skill typologies that it's understandable to feel overwhelmed. To further complicate things, different organizations, researchers, and curriculum companies often use different terms for the same skills. Some people—even educators—hold strong opinions about preferred terms that can hamper idea sharing and securing buy-in from peers. I believe that making any terms forbidden leaves the entire concept seemingly untouchable.

SEL skills can be referred to as 21st-century skills, employability skills, behavioral skills, essential skills, soft skills, life skills, and more. For me, it doesn't matter what they are called if there's a shared understanding of and enthusiasm for the knowledge, skills, and attitudes being prioritized. If a common understanding is developed within your school or organization's setting, it should be adopted widely and reflect your vision, mission, and community. If you're pursuing this on your own, choose a framework whose language resonates with you.

I encourage you not to get bogged down in the variances within SEL. That energy is better spent internalizing content and preparing to integrate it into your classroom experience. The following two frameworks will exemplify how these skills are typically organized. An "SEL Vignette" follows each competency or durable skill dimension. These vignettes were gleaned from research with teachers, learners, and families, or they were drafted based on my lived experiences in various educational settings. Each will shed light on SEL education in action. Where possible, the ideas listed in the SEL vignettes are included in the Resource Guide.

The CASEL 5: Core SEL Competencies

CASEL has a set of five core competencies to organize its approach to SEL. The competencies, called "the CASEL 5," are Self-Awareness, Self-Management, Social Awareness, Relationship Skills, and Responsible Decision-Making. Each is further described using related skills. Figure 3.1 shows the CASEL Wheel, framing how the core competencies are embedded into several essential contexts in which students live. The information that follows can be found on CASEL's webpage: `www.casel.org`, which is also linked in the Resource Guide.

Figure 3.2 outlines skills that flesh out CASEL 5.

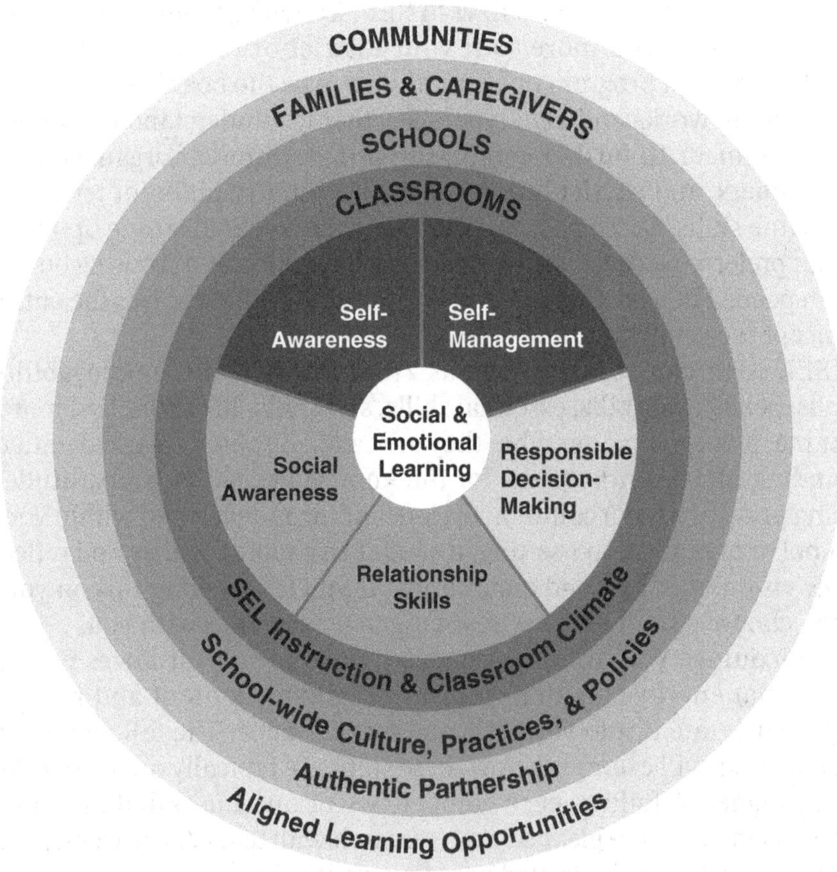

Figure 3.1: The CASEL Wheel.

Self-Awareness	Self-Management	Social Awareness	Relationship Skills	Responsible Decision-Making
■ Identifying emotions and thoughts ■ Accurate self-perception ■ Recognizing strengths ■ Self-confidence ■ Self-efficacy ■ Growth mindset	■ Self-regulation and impulse control ■ Stress management ■ Self-discipline ■ Self-motivation ■ Goal-setting ■ Organizational skills	■ Perspective-taking ■ Empathy ■ Appreciating diversity ■ Respect for others ■ Understanding of cultural and ethical norms	■ Communication skills ■ Social engagement ■ Relationship-building ■ Teamwork ■ Resist inappropriate social pressures ■ Conflict resolution ■ Supportive behaviors	■ Problem identification ■ Situation analysis ■ Problem solving ■ Evaluating ■ Reflecting ■ Ethical responsibility

Figure 3.2: Social and emotional competencies and related skills as defined by CASEL.

Self-Awareness

This is defined by CASEL as "The ability to accurately recognize one's emotions and thoughts and their influence on behavior. This includes accurately assessing one's strengths and limitations and possessing a well-grounded sense of confidence and optimism." As teachers, we can encourage students to take time out to reflect on their thoughts, emotions, and behaviors. Guided journaling or in-class exercises can support this. Self-awareness also encourages a student to bring their values front of mind. Consider a journal prompt that asks, "What values, for example, justice, safety, tradition, and courtesy, are most important to me?" The reflection process that supports self-awareness doesn't have to be vocal or public to be effective.

When students identify and understand their personal values, they are in a far stronger position to pursue the right career fit—a job that suits their character. What's more, if students are in touch with their emotions, understand their own minds, and how their actions and behaviors impact both themselves and others, this Self-awareness helps them connect and cooperate with others in a variety of settings. Reflection genuinely fuels the learning process as students can identify what is and is not working for them. They also better recognize and understand their strengths and weaknesses. This learning creates a virtuous cycle that self-fulfills, as reflection builds a confident sense of self, "I know who I am," and self-efficacy, "I can do this." Becoming self-aware is an excellent place to kickstart an SEL journey as it helps to leverage and open the door to everything that follows.

SELF-AWARENESS IN THE WORKPLACE

Giving and Receiving Feedback – Feedback is a part of all professions. Demonstrating Self-Awareness on the job means naming one's own strengths and areas of growth. Self-aware individuals walk into feedback conversations ready to share specific examples of their strong performance and identify their struggles. Naming concrete steps towards improved job performance reflects another level of self-awareness. Highly self-aware individuals can also remain receptive to feedback on their blind spots, which are, by definition, unknowable in advance. Remaining open to feedback is a type of Self-Awareness that nurtures growth.

Responsibility to your Team – Self-aware individuals recognize the impact of their choices. For example, regularly leaving early from or asking to reschedule a meeting because "something came up" indicates a lack of Self-Awareness relative to one's group responsibility. The result is missed opportunity for collaboration. Someone is missing out on important conversations, and the group is missing contributions from a team member.

Adapting to Change – For better or worse, change is a constant in the workplace. Planned change occurs over time, or rapid changes comes on suddenly. Self-awareness in a changing environment means noticing change and noticing one's response to change. In the face of change, self-aware individuals understand their contribution, for better or worse, to that change.

Self-Management

This is defined by CASEL as "The ability to regulate one's emotions, thoughts, and behaviors effectively in different situations. This includes managing stress, controlling impulses, motivating oneself, and setting and working toward achieving personal and academic goals." Consider the difference between a loud, explosive three-year-old child who feels every emotion, impulse, and desire intensely and a sage elder who can move between joy, sympathy, fear, and wonder without breaking a sweat. Most of our learners fall somewhere in the middle, just as we ourselves do, quite frankly. Controlling our emotions and managing our short- and long-term motivations can make all the difference when personal goals are on the line.

On any given day, students need to resist an array of impulses. They must delay immediate gratification in big and small ways. They must balance their long-term goals against what must happen in the immediate future. These requirements aren't new. Learning to manage yourself has always been a huge part of growing up. Yet, in today's highly digitized world, young people are susceptible to a new range of impulsive distractions—social media notifications, video games, streaming YouTube videos, and so on. Each of these diversions has been scientifically designed to grab and hold attention.

Beyond the influence of modern technology, students may experience problems in their home environments that they are completely not responsible for creating. The possibilities are endless: it could be a relationship breakdown between the student's parents or caregivers, financial concerns, household responsibilities, or even lacking the privacy needed to move through puberty and concentrate on their studies. Teachers and trainers may or may not know the full story their students carry into class each day, and we may never fully know. Yet for students to excel in their studies and successfully transition to the workforce, they need to manage, and ultimately, overcome these distractions and challenges to sustain efforts toward their goals. A student who can manage their attention, motivation, and emotions is poised to organize themselves, embody resilience, and succeed in life and work.

SELF-MANAGEMENT IN THE WORKPLACE

Self-Management follows Self-Awareness. Only self-aware individuals are truly capable of self-management. Demonstrating self-management through self-regulation, impulse control and self-motivation on the job can make the difference between keeping a job or getting fired, to put it bluntly. Time and again on jobsites across the world, supervisors tell me about individuals who need hounding to complete tasks or who need to be terminated for losing their cool. I've learned that just about every job has very stressful or very mundane tasks... or both! Like my dad always tells me, "That's why they call it a J-O-B." Self-management helps us navigate these inevitable and frustrating moments. We all need to develop a toolbox for navigating the less-than-enjoyable moments of work. At the end of the day, self-management is about lifelong learning and remaining open to reskilling. Managing stress and controlling impulses leads towards motivating oneself and working towards personal and professional goals.

Social Awareness

This is defined by CASEL as "The ability to take the perspective of and empathize with others from diverse backgrounds and cultures, to understand social and ethical norms for behavior, and to recognize family, school, and community resources and supports."

Where Self-awareness focuses on one's own emotions and thoughts, Social Awareness draws attention to our abilities to account for the emotions and thoughts of others. Humans are social creatures; no one lives and works in a vacuum. Our students must extend their awareness beyond the self to those they interact with—their peers, teachers, employers, and communities. Perspective-taking allows students to see the world through the eyes of others and increases empathy. No community nor society is monolithic. Diversity is everywhere; increased Self-awareness will foster inclusion, and increased inclusion allows more significant opportunities for everyone to thrive—not just those most in need of it. Mutual respect, understanding norms, and social cooperation are vital to enable thriving and diverse classrooms and workplaces.

SOCIAL AWARENESS IN THE WORKPLACE

Individuals with strong Social Awareness work well with others. When I shadowed cyber security professionals, I was shocked to learn that empathy was a core skill needed for high performance. When combined with emotional Self-Awareness, empathetic cyber security professionals were able to keep cool when dealing with an overwhelming number of customers scammed by fake or "phishing" emails. Empathizing with less computer-savvy employees made them more effective and maintained a calm, focused environment. When working with sales professionals, I learned firsthand how far an empathetic salesperson can go. Other critical aspects of Social Awareness are related to appreciating diverse cultural and ethical norms and acting equitably in the face of difference. Working for a global organization, this aspect of Social Awareness hits home for me. Each individual presents uniquely, and teams are incredibly diverse. Taking time to learn about others' cultural and ethical norms goes a long way.

Relationship Skills

This is defined by CASEL as "The ability to establish and maintain healthy and rewarding relationships with diverse individuals and groups. This includes communicating clearly, listening actively, cooperating, resisting inappropriate social pressure, negotiating conflict constructively, and seeking and offering help when needed." The heart of this competency is being able to thrive in relationships with others. From friendships to family relationships to employer relationships, this skill set supports learners in nearly every aspect of their lives.

In many ways, this core competency builds on Social Awareness. Socially aware students also need specific capabilities to develop effective relationships. Every good relationship, whether in the classroom, in a community, or in the workplace, is built through communication—verbal and nonverbal, face-to-face, and now more than ever, digital. When communication doesn't go as planned, and misunderstandings arise, other Relationship Skills like handling conflict and seeking help come into play. The intersection of Social Awareness and Relationship Skills covers the knowledge, skills, and aptitudes needed to thrive in lasting, meaningful relationships with a variety of people and face conflict and challenge without sacrificing connection.

Connection and teamwork are, after all, the crux of nearly all companies and organizations. Very few students will choose careers where they don't interact with others on a regular basis. Relationship-building demands resiliency and the ability to negotiate and overcome conflict, including in the workplace. Teamwork, after all, is the essential "glue" that allows individuals and organizations to get things done well.

RELATIONSHIP SKILLS IN THE WORKPLACE

In most professions, we spend more time with our coworkers than our families. Even for individuals who work independently most of the time, such as call center agents or bank tellers, social engagement is vital to effective work. When creating training programs, I host focus groups with high performers and low performers on the job. We often talk about their coworkers – the "adult drama" that can all too often make for a toxic workplace. The high performers on the job consistently speak about how they confront and resolve situations that create a toxic environment. Teaching professional Relationship Skills early on can help prevent students from succumbing to this pitfall of modern workplace culture. Learning how to resist inappropriate social pressures on the job is as critical as it is in middle- and high-school. When students learn conflict resolution skills and supportive social behaviors such as listening with empathy, communicating with clarity, and cooperating towards shared goals, everyone thrives.

Responsible Decision-Making

This is defined by CASEL as "The ability to make constructive and respectful choices about personal behavior and social interactions based on consideration of ethical standards, safety concerns, social norms, the realistic evaluation of consequences of various actions, and the well-being of self and others." I'm struck by the image of a frustrated parent looking at their child who just drew all over their bedroom walls with crayons. "You know better than this!" the parent cries with their hand in the air. Responsible Decision-Making bridges the gap between knowing better and doing better.

Students face an array of decisions every day, some mundane, some amusing, and some meaningful. Some of these decisions are ethical in nature. For instance, a student may witness her classmates mocking a student who has a different accent. The student notices everyone is laughing at the teased student, and no one is intervening. Does she speak up and risk being mocked herself? Does she commit to connecting with the bullied peer later, after the fact? Does she do nothing? The myriad inputs, considerations, and possibilities she uses to make her decision—often in the blink of an eye—fall under the umbrella of Responsible Decision-Making.

Regardless of whether decisions are morally significant, both educators and employers expect students and employees to be ready and able to make optimal decisions. This competency goes beyond understanding problems; students also require the confidence to solve them. These problem-solving abilities don't rely solely on analysis and evaluation. Students must also successfully navigate decisions while honoring their own moral codes, the expectations of their employer, and the social needs of those around them.

RESPONSIBLE DECISION MAKING IN THE WORKPLACE

When visiting manufacturing plants, I was blown away by the amount of safety protocols and signage. I was required to attend safety training before even walking out onto the floor. Supervisors constantly stress the importance of safety. In workplaces where there is heavy machinery, not following a safety protocol can be a matter of life or death. Supervisors often shared with me that new workers would push back on wearing safety gear. "It is hot," or "I forgot it," or "It's not such a big deal." The consequence for repeatedly failing to wear proper safety gear could be your job, either by termination or by injury. Supervisors relay that most accidents happen when someone isn't properly wearing safety gear and when rushing to finish before lunch or quitting time. Even in less physically dangerous environments, such as the office, Responsible Decision Making is vital. Whether it be related to social and cultural norms or professional ethical standards, the highest performing workers tend to make good decisions based on a realistic evaluation of the consequences of various actions.

Durable Skills Framework

Like the CASEL 5, the Durable Skills framework from America Succeeds is a well-researched and popular framework for understanding essential SEL skills. America Succeeds is a nonprofit that bridges the education policy and business sectors to further their vision to help "public education systems prepare every student to succeed in the competitive global economy and contribute to their local community." Many high schools and workforce development programs use this framework to increase adoption and application of the 10 Durable Skills featured in their framework. The nonprofit's work is rooted in the belief that these skills are necessary to secure and maintain employment, both now and in the changing days ahead.

Since its inception in 2014, America Succeeds has brought together thousands of stakeholders, including employers, policymakers, and educators. One way they've done this is through Age of Agility Summits, where roundtable discussions lead to recommendations and policy guidance addressing the education sector's challenges in enhancing graduate employability. Critical issues that have crossed stakeholders' desks include preparing our students for the workplace when artificial intelligence and robots are changing so many roles, as well as the business sector's difficulties in finding and hiring qualified workers with SEL competencies.

A fundamental learning from these pioneering efforts is the recognition that while so-called "hard" skills are essential, the SEL skills covered in this chapter are deemed even more critical for employability. America Succeeds notes that, "The Analysis of 80 million job postings from 2020–2021 reveals that 7 of the 10 most-requested skills are Durable Skills. And, the top 5 Durable Skills were requested in job postings 4.7 times more often than the top 5 hard skills" (Cole et al., 2021).

Employability undergirds everything the Durable Skills framework represents. An obvious added benefit is that these skills are many of the same ones educators want to instill in learners so they can become fully actualized and thriving adults.

What Are Durable Skills?

The Durable Skills framework (see Figures 3.3 and 3.4) includes many different types of SEL skills. To make sense of these diverse skills, America Succeeds organizes Durable Skills across 10 dimensions. The nonprofit offers a high-level definition of that dimension before sharing discrete skills and traits that work together to show competency in that dimension. A link for reading more directly from "America Succeeds" is included in the Resource Guide. Each dimension can offer inroads, insights, and inspiration as you consider how to improve SEL education in your class or training center.

Leadership	**Character**	**Collaboration**
Directing efforts and delivering results	Personal and professional conduct	Teamwork and connection
Thought Leadership	Professionalism	Interpersonal Communications
Leadership Development	Enthusiasm	Coordinating
Risk Management	Accountability	Teamwork
Advocacy	High Motivation	Scheduling
Project Management	Trustworthiness	Team Oriented
Influencing Skills	Tactfulness	Team Leadership
Decision-Making	Reliability	Collaboration
Mentorship	Ethical Conduct	Team Building
Leadership	Social Skills	Cooperation
Management	High Integrity	Virtual Teams

Communication	**Creativity**
Information exchange and management	New ideas and novel solutions
Communications	Innovation
Presentations	Creativity
Written Communication	Creative Problem-Solving
Verbal Communication Skills	Creative Thinking
Negotiation	Imagination
Multilingualism	Visionary
Public Relations	Ingenuity
Social Media	Ideation
Persuasive Communication	Experimentation
Public Speaking	Brainstorming

Figure 3.3: Durable Skills 1–5: dimensions, definitions, and examples.

Critical Thinking	Metacognition	Mindfulness
Informed ideas and effective solutions	Self-understanding and personal management	Interpersonal and self-awareness
■ Problem Solving	■ Constructive Feedback	■ Culturally Sensitive
■ Research	■ Multitasking	■ Humility
■ Troubleshooting	■ Goal-Setting	■ Emotional Intelligence
■ Prioritization	■ Diplomacy	■ Active Listening
■ Investigation	■ Adaptability	■ Listening Skills
■ Data Analysis	■ Time Management	■ Patience
■ Critical Thinking	■ Organizational Skills	■ Empathy
■ Intellectual Curiosity	■ Teaching	■ Customer Relationship Management
■ Complex Problem Solving	■ Planning	■ Compassion
■ Analytical Thinking	■ Detail Orientated	■ Hospitality

Growth Mindset	Fortitude
Improvement and aspiration	Constitution and inspiration
■ Self-Sufficiency	■ Self-Confident
■ Results Focused	■ Calmness under Pressure
■ Action Oriented	■ Persistence
■ Entrepreneurship	■ Team Motivation
■ Goal Oriented	■ Self-Discipline
■ Resourcefulness	■ Assertiveness
■ Curiosity	■ Tenacity
■ Proactivity	■ Optimism
■ Strategic Planning	■ Motivational Skills
■ Self-Starter	■ Resilience

Figure 3.4: Durable Skills 6–10: dimensions, definitions, and examples.

Leadership

Leaders are not born; leaders are made. And as educators, we are privileged to play an important role in shaping tomorrow's leaders. Unsurprisingly, decision-making falls under the Leadership skill category. CASEL's framework emphasizes that adopting a responsible mindset toward decisions is essential. Advocacy, persuasion, influence, and project management contribute to workplace readiness because leadership is a desirable trait, even if the initial role at a company does not involve direct leadership over teammates or projects.

Students can start fostering their own leadership by managing and influencing their own behaviors. Group projects, part-time jobs, school clubs, and sports teams offer safe places to further grow skills that help motivate and steer others. As educators, we need to help our learners recognize and pursue leadership by continually and explicitly linking their work with leadership skills.

SEL VIGNETTE: LEADERSHIP

Liam was in his freshman year at a university, and he was signed up for a coaching and mentoring course. He was excited as it was a fantastic opportunity to mentor school students aged 15 to 17 at a local school. It wasn't so long ago that he left school himself, but he was eager to practice and learn how to mentor like a true leader.

After all, he kept reading about how so many jobs would soon be replaced by automation and artificial intelligence, and Liam understood that transformational leadership demanded excellent communication skills, the ability to influence others, and taking the lead in sharing innovative thoughts and ideas. During the term, he regularly visited the local school and practiced his mentoring skills.

He also noticed something else about this unique experience. He recognized genuine progress in his mentees. It wasn't just him who was benefitting from this. And like a chain reaction, in noticing that, his capacity for empathy is also increasing.

When based on real- life people, all personal and school names in SEL Vignettes have been changed to ensure anonymity.

Character

Good character has always been desirable. Employers have long sought to evaluate their employees' reliability, trustworthiness, and accountability during the interview process. Today's job marketplace is no different. Work ethic, integrity, tact, and ethical conduct are precious traits that are hard for employers to instill after the point of hire.

However, frustrations arise when a job seeker overestimates themself in terms of these traits. Someone's personal level of professionalism, for example, is hard to quantify given it's difficult to see ourselves objectively. According to survey data from the National Association of Colleges and Employers (2021), students rate their own work ethic much higher (89.4%) than employers rate recent graduates (42.5%).

This wide gap is problematic—especially as job seekers graduating from college don't realize it exists. We must temper our students' overconfidence and give them the tools and language for more objectively understanding themselves. Linking back to CASEL's framework, Self-Awareness will prove pivotal in character-building and meeting employers' expectations.

Character, as categorized by America Succeeds, covers a breadth of in-demand abilities and traits from social and interpersonal skills to motivation. Even casual glances at job postings show that employers are looking for well-rounded, self-aware, job-ready joiners of good character.

SEL VIGNETTE: CHARACTER

Bashir is a recent graduate from a top university. With a GPA score of 4.0, he nailed his degree. Yet, unlike his peers, he was not getting past the interview stage.

While Bashir's job applications earned him many interview requests, he started to wonder if his character was not coming across well. He invested in several LinkedIn® courses, such as "Creating Great First Impressions," but needed extra help. With so many rejections under his belt, his confidence had taken a hit. However, he drummed up the courage to ask his old dissertation advisor for assistance.

They both decided on doing a video-recorded mock interview for analysis. This process helped raise self-awareness of how his character came across—he wasn't enthusiastic, and his storytelling skills lacked persuasion. He also wasn't highlighting experiences or anecdotes that demonstrated his true character—that he's someone who does the right thing when it's hard to do, someone who was always willing to go the extra mile.

With this new self-awareness and a hunger to show off who he really is, Bashir recorded himself practicing interview questions. He evaluated himself, and had friends help to see if he was coming off as he intended to. He asked his friends, "When you watch this, does it feel like the real me is showing up?" After a few weeks of practice and reflection, it didn't take long for him to land his dream role.

Collaboration

In most industries, in most roles, work gets done through connecting with others and maximizing teamwork. Every job demands collaboration, and it's a skill high on every employer's wish list. While our educational institutions are communities, studying can sometimes feel like a lonely experience. In the end, we sit for exams by ourselves, earn grades by ourselves, and face life after graduation by ourselves.

Most teachers create opportunities for collaborative teamwork in the form of projects, labs, or other complex assignments. Yet teamwork opportunities are not necessarily enough for collaboration to work well. Collaboration is notoriously tricky, and teams often don't work as well as they could.

The key to successful teamwork lies in a team's culture, and culture can be actively created and fostered. Have no doubt, without active intention, culture will evolve on its own organically. But students can build habits that lead to intentionality with regard to building culture, understanding their own needs on a team as well as the needs of teammates, and supporting each other with trust and accountability. More importantly, nurturing a sense of psychological safety, where everyone feels safe and free of judgment, is the "secret" ingredient. When psychological safety is in place, everyone can more easily actively listen and effectively collaborate.

SEL VIGNETTE: COLLABORATION

Erica headed up an apprenticeship program within her computer engineering firm. She was keen to develop both up-and-coming talent and high-performing teams through apprenticeships. She sensed some of the apprentices weren't feeling as connected to the team as she would have liked.

Erica decided to host an "Uncover the Stinky Fish (Before it Rots)" event. This involved an anonymous visual tool that allowed team members to expose issues they were struggling with but in a silent and anonymous way. With everyone in the same room, it quickly became apparent that several members felt intimidated by some overly dominant characters among her apprentices. These feelings were most acute among young women, introverts, and ethnic minority apprentices.

She was eager to make everyone feel integral to their team's success, she arranged a suite of workshops and teamwork "rules" to increase psychological safety over the coming year. Activities ranged from hosting coffee chats to implementing a "No-Interruptions" rule during regular check-ins to promote psychological safety.

Communication

Speaking, listening, reading, writing: four essential components of one of life's most important skills—Communication. On the job, students need to master skills as varied as giving presentations, report writing, interacting with the public, social media marketing, negotiation, persuasion, and more.

Our education system has long provided learning opportunities to develop communication skills. Communication, like critical thinking, is one part of SEL that our profession embraced long ago. Yet there's a disconnect at play; employers consistently report that students fall short on many of these critical Communication skills. As our world evolves, the nature of and context in which we train for these skills must also evolve. Information is everywhere, and talk is cheap. AI is now capable of writing reports, synthesizing information, and answering questions on demand. How should we adapt our skills to working with and alongside technology like this? The answer will emerge, and soon, and our methods and expectations around the teaching and learning of communication skills must adapt when it does.

One important aspect of communication skills worth emphasizing is adapting to meet an audience's needs. Tailoring communication takes practice and can be tricky for younger job seekers who communicate casually via text messages, emojis, memes, and videos. Adaptive communication is an "unlock" for many students. It's incredible to witness a student get their message across by knowing the audience. Whether it's written, verbal, or shared via body language, adaptive communicators understand how to effectively transmit their values, message, or topic stance.

SEL VIGNETTE: COMMUNICATION

Ian was a university professor who worked with the Earth Sciences faculty. He felt blessed to work with young curious minds, and he loved his job! But he had long felt that his students' presentation skills were lacking. As communication skills were crucial for employability, he wanted to develop their storytelling skills.

Ian knew that science can come across as dry and boring to some people. And whether his learners will choose careers in the Earth Sciences or not, he knew that telling a story well is a powerful tool. He decided to embed a presentation requirement into his course's mid-term assessment, but with a twist. The presentation event used a TED style format. What's more, he invited the local community to join the audience. To give the students a confidence boost, he invited faculty from the arts and humanities to provide some pre-event training.

This combination proved a winning formula. While nervous at the outset, the students enjoyed their novel learning experience. Even better, they gained encouraging yet constructive feedback from their local community.

Creativity

Employers demand innovative young minds as labor and capital alone are insufficient to stay competitive in today's global marketplace. Creativity in schools often starts with musical or artistic expression, but that's just the beginning. Unexpected solutions to math problems, engaging ways to interact with peers during group work, a bold and surprising idea to take their social studies projects out into the community—these actions involve leadership and courage, to be sure. But they start with creativity skills

Unfortunately, we often hear children—and adults—say, "I'm just not a creative person." A long debunked neuromyth about left-brained and right-brained attributes sometimes gives false credence to a claim about a person's inherent abilities to create. Teachers need to spread the word—everyone can grow their creative skills, especially when we think of creativity beyond visual and musical art. (The same is true for the "I'm not a math person" falsehood that still gets traction in schools, families, and workplaces). One simple solution is for educators to evaluate their current projects and activities through the lens of creativity. Identify moments of creation, name it, and celebrate learners who dig in. The more our students are told they are creative, the more they will believe it and live it.

SEL VIGNETTE: CREATIVITY

Devon was a college sophomore studying computer science. He was a whizz at programming and had lost count of the number of times he had been called left-brained. Writing code and understanding computers had always come easily to him.

So, Devon was stumped when one of his professors arranged a workshop to apply the projective visual expressive technique—a market research technique to understand consumer perceptions of brands. His task? To better understand the PC market. At first, he resisted. "Surely a market research survey could do the job better?"

But he rolled up his sleeves to give it a go. His task was to create a collage out of magazine cut-outs, and he created pictures to capture a brand's "personality." To his surprise, Michael was pleased with his expressive interpretation. Even better, it was fun, and he found himself pondering surprising questions while he, literally, cut and pasted pieces to his collage. The images he kept seeing for his assigned brand gave him inspiration to doodle his own computer case.

Critical Thinking

This durable skill starts with informed thinking and ends with effective solutions. Tucked into the qualifier *informed* is the need to evaluate and prioritize information rather than accepting things at face value; questioning has long been critical. This is more important than ever as we live in a "post-truth" world where facts, opinions, and falsehoods are hard to differentiate.

Employers are thrilled when a new hire demonstrates the ability to identify the root cause of a problem, brainstorm creative options, and deliver solutions either on their own or—better—through collaborating with a team. The confidence and ability to do just that sets candidates apart during the hiring processes.

The ability to process inputs rationally and arrive at solutions that make sense and deliver results—that's the heart of Critical Thinking skills.

SEL VIGNETTE: CRITICAL THINKING

Maritza was a middle school art teacher. Keen to integrate critical thinking into her classroom, she decided to hold a debate on "Can art be objectively perceived?" Knowing her students, she sensed opinions differed.

Maritza opted for the barometer exercise. Before the activity got underway, she organized a contract with her students; to avoid any outbursts, respect was their No. 1 rule. She also gave them tips on how to disagree constructively, for example, encouraging "I" statements rather than accusatory "you" statements.

With a contract and constructive supports in place, students then "Took a Stand" with their prepared opinion by taking a position along a U-shape made of masking tape on the floor; the opposite ends of the continuum were marked "Strongly Agree" and "Strongly Disagree." Students moved up and down the continuum sharing their opinions. As students were encouraged to back up their arguments with evidence, quite a few students shifted from their initial positions. What was particularly notable was their Critical Thinking skills—respect ruled the debate, and everyone learned something new.

Metacognition

Being able to analyze how you think, act, and create accelerates personal growth. This durable skill dimension directly connects with CASEL's emphasis on Self-Awareness. The importance of self-monitoring is not mentioned verbatim in the Durable Skills framework, but it is connected to the skills attached to metacognition: time management, organizational skills, goal-setting. When students develop the skill to self-monitor how they are doing, they gain greater insight into how and to what extent they are making progress.

"Thinking about thinking" connects two sides of the same coin—knowledge and regulation. A metacognitively aware learner will have a sense of what they know and don't know; they will also be aware, for example, via evaluating their performance, how well they are planning, and reaching their goals. Together, this metacognitive awareness helps students perform better academically and gives job seekers the edge they need to succeed in the workplace.

SEL VIGNETTE: METACOGNITION

Bianca was a highly conscientious medical student and was busy juggling a considerable workload. But instead of being busy, she longed to be productive. That way, she would have more time for leisure and boost her well-being.

She got a couple of apps to help self-monitor her activities. Bianca used one app that monitors all her desktop and mobile activities—she realized that maybe scrolling through TikTok isn't a good idea during her workday. It's not that she was spending much time on it; instead, she noticed it took her too much time to get back into her work after a social media break.

Now Bianca takes a stroll around the local park to clear her head. She also has a free habit-tracking app. This helps her realize she isn't drinking enough water. Now that she's hydrated and taking better breaks, she's getting 20% more done in less time. Moreover, her thought processes are less muddled, and inspiration regularly strikes.

Mindfulness

Those who are truly mindful enjoy and benefit from a compassionate awareness of others and the self. Mindfulness connects to CASEL's framework—for instance, compassion, empathy, and emotional intelligence. Mindfulness involves active listening, a hugely important skill to nurture in our students. Everyone engages in communication—some say we spend up to 80% of our workday communicating with others in one form or another. Yet very little of this time involves active listening, despite the fact that we are born with two ears and one mouth. All told, those with the ability to pay respectful attention to what others say and feel are in short supply nowadays. Yet active listening is something we can teach and learn, like any other skill.

Cultural sensitivity is also enhanced with mindfulness skills. Why? It serves as a bridge between our awareness of cultural differences and our responses to them. While not mentioned explicitly in the Durable Skills framework, the same could be said for neurodiversity. When we are actively listening to others, we stand a far greater chance of noticing the influence of our own biases and attending to them "in the moment" to prevent both harm and misunderstandings. Mindfulness is also a tool that helps with self-regulation. When we teach students to be mindful to their current thoughts, emotions, and feelings, this gives them the momentary presence to keep them in check.

SEL VIGNETTE: MINDFULNESS

Tom was a twelfth-grade mathematics teacher. As the exam season approached, it felt like Groundhog Day. Every year it was the same—stress levels rose, conflict broke out between students, and behavioral problems were not uncommon.

Having attended an SEL training course, Tom knew about the Active Listening Conversation Partners exercise. He decided to put the idea into action. He paired a student with a different conversation partner each time and invited both to share, in turn, what was on their mind. Once their partner finished sharing, the student paraphrased what their partner told them, normally starting with, "It sounds like . . ." When it was appropriate, the partners would ask questions of each other.

It was a quick exercise that he now regularly slots into class, both during exam season and during low-stress parts of year. During the exam period, though, Tom noticed that students were expressing empathy, body language was more open, and judgmental comments were far less frequent.

Growth Mindset

Social psychologist Carol Dweck published *Mindset: The New Psychology of Success* in 2006, and ever since, the concepts of growth and fixed mindset have helped educators, trainers, and students open their minds to the possibility that skills, habits of mind, and capabilities can be developed. When we work hard, embrace challenges, and learn from our mistakes, we can improve. Growth mindset contrasts with a fixed mindset, wherein a person believes capabilities are fixed—either within themselves or others. Consider the neuromyth we covered earlier when reviewing creativity: "I'm just not a creative person." Because a person with a fixed mindset believes talent is innate and cannot be improved, looking smart can take precedence over being smart because you don't think you can be smart if you aren't already! This inauthenticity often works against one's self-awareness, metacognition, and leadership.

When learners and their teachers believe they can grow if they commit time and energy toward acquiring knowledge and practicing new skills, personal evolution is the result. Therefore, a growth mindset is a powerful accelerator when aiming to acquire and master Durable Skills.

For nearly 20 years, education publishers have tried to harness growth mindset for commercial gain. There are colorful growth mindset charts and snazzy-looking activities for teachers to use. Alone, they aren't enough to instill growth mindset into a learner's sense of self. Materials, activities, and session plans will never overcome the impact of teachers who don't believe in growth mindset themselves. When educators do believe in it, model it, and invoke it when interacting with students, doors open and magic can happen.

SEL VIGNETTE: GROWTH MINDSET

Casandra was at risk of becoming a university dropout. Nearly 40% of college students fail to graduate at two-year colleges and end up saddled with debt without the benefits of a degree. She feared she might become another such learner, but she wasn't sure what to do about it. She constantly felt down in the dumps—a few missed deadlines here, some failing grades there. She just wasn't performing well across the board. She had daydreams about dropping out and leaving the stress of college academics behind her.

One of her professors noticed Casandra's slipping performance and invited her for a chat during office hours. Casandra nearly didn't go; she couldn't see the point. But she's so glad she did now. She discovered that her current performance, and her abilities, weren't fixed at all. Her professor walked her through the basics of a fixed versus growth mindset, and in doing so, lit a fire within her.

Casandra accepted an invitation to attend some mindset workshops. She learned about the brain's plasticity and how challenge and failure can fuel progress and winning performances. Change didn't happen overnight, but over the coming months, Casandra's attitude and performance showed dramatic improvements. Casandra graduated on time with an associate's degree and now wants to apply for a bachelor's degree program. She's also landed a great interim role as a part-time junior account executive in music marketing, a great way to reduce her student debt and strengthen her résumé at the same time.

Fortitude

No matter the role, and no matter the industry, every young person faces a professional journey that will have bumps in the road. From unsupportive bosses to unexpected layoffs to overtime before a big deadline to personal conflict with peers—when the going to gets tough, some shine and some falter. Fortitude is the difference maker in many situations.

I want to talk about the "Valley of Disappointment," a concept created by James Clear, the best-selling author of *Atomic Habits*. This phenomenon helps students understand why there's the temptation to give up early when situations feel insurmountable. Progress toward a goal is rarely linear. In other words, progress is not directly proportional to the invested effort in over time, even though we think it should be. Instead, it's normal for progress to kick in midway through a project, or later. Meanwhile, it seems like no progress is being made at all. Clear calls the space between what we expected to happen and what has actually happened the "Valley of Disappointment." It is illustrated in Figure 3.5. Unmet expectations often lead to frustrations and a loss of motivation.

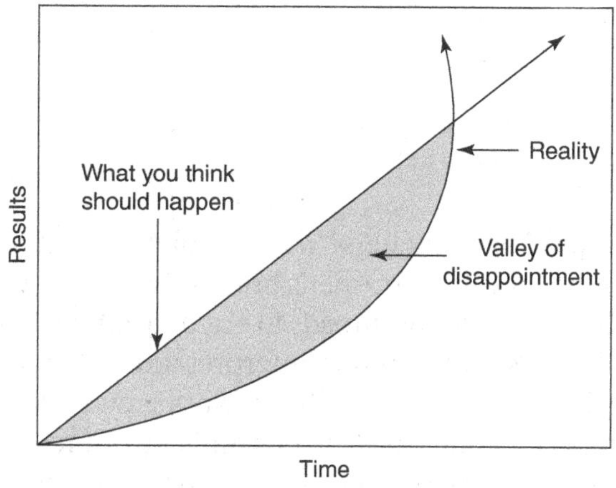

Figure 3.5: The Valley of Disappointment.

Source: James Clear, *Atomic Habits*.

Luckily, we don't stay in the valley forever. Progress and outcomes await those who don't quit, reflect often, and change course as necessary. Optimism, resilience, self-confidence, and self-motivation are key skills for staying the course against headwinds like perceived initial failure, unexpected hardships, and critical peers.

SEL VIGNETTE: FORTITUDE

Shanice was recently accepted onto an apprenticeship program but felt overwhelmed and uncertain. She is a caretaker for her single mom who has multiple sclerosis. Shanice herself was struggling with anxiety and depression. Worried she'd blow her chances of doing well as an apprentice, she sought psychological help.

She knew that she couldn't change her mother's condition, and she knew she would not abandon her mother no matter how hard their situation together was. After several visits with her psychologist, she recognized the need to reframe stress to gain the resilience and fortitude to keep going. She read the book *The Upside of Stress*, authored by Stanford lecturer Kelly McGonigal. She also watched the professor's TED talk on "How to Make Stress Your Friend."

Over several months, Shanice's ability to cope with stress increased, slowly at first and then significantly. She couldn't change her mom's situation, but she did come to see her difficult situation through a new lens. This newfound fortitude helped her move forward with her apprenticeship.

Closing Thoughts on Social and Emotional Learning

Social-Emotional Learning helps make explicit the knowledge, skills, and attributes that develop a learner's humanity alongside their technical abilities. It offers tremendous inroads to building employability skills and much more. Yet it is quite open to interpretation. Though there is considerable overlap between the two frameworks reviewed in this chapter, each framework does have its own lens and body of research to support that lens, and there are myriad other frameworks you can investigate. The development of SEL skills doesn't always play out linearly, and isolating one can feel strange as, truly, the skills are all interconnected.

By way of example, self-awareness is unlikely to ever be achieved via self-reflection alone. Instead, feedback-seeking is also essential to get the "bigger picture." But feedback can be quite hard to handle. If your classroom or training center has not yet established an abiding sense of safety for all learners, sharing and receiving feedback will be an uphill climb. Even more difficult will be instilling a humble and curious spirit in your learners so they continue to seek out feedback in future settings. Learning how to accept feedback well is critical to success in the world. So, in addition to self-reflection, a focused effort to build muscles for giving and receiving feedback is all required—which requires its own set of prerequisites.

Moreover, consider the need for positive self-reflection, as many students experience mental health issues. There's a fine line between reflection and rumination, and too much reflection could cause a negative spiral in mental well-being. We must tell our students that reflection and receiving feedback are positive activities. And to reap the benefits of self-awareness, we must approach reflection with compassion and an open mind—and a bias toward action. Constant reflection without intention to evolve falls flat, and constantly berating yourself and calling it "reflection" will not support growth.

Getting the correct dose of reflection hints at my second caveat. Building SEL skills is not necessarily achieved in linear proportion. Let's consider confidence briefly. If a learner experiences too little confidence, they will struggle to put themselves forward. Yet, too much confidence is likely to rebound. Research shows that when we're overconfident, we are far more likely to take inappropriate risks and make faulty decisions. Organizational psychologist Adam Grant wrote a best-selling book, *Think Again,* wherein he warns against overconfidence. He notes that studies find that, "the people who scored the lowest on an emotional intelligence test weren't just the most likely to overestimate their skills. They were also the most likely to dismiss their scores as inaccurate or irrelevant—and the least likely to invest in coaching or self-improvement." Instead, we need to look for the Goldilocks effect—just the right amount of confidence! The same can be said for productivity. Yes, we want entrepreneurial students to become self-sufficient and results oriented. But we don't want our students to be so overproductive that they risk burnout. Given the need for balance, as educators, we must encourage skills such as fortitude while ensuring our students get the right balance.

It is best to not think of SEL as a laundry list of skills, instead to name, nurture and teach their interconnectedness.

It's also noteworthy that while the need for inclusive, Durable Skills-based education and hiring was long apparent before the pandemic, Covid-19 significantly accelerated existing trends. As we look toward economic recovery—and overcoming the inequities exacerbated by these past years—it is even more critical to ensure every individual is prepared or upskilled with the social and emotional skills necessary for long-term success in the workforce. By focusing on common competencies as well as diverse technical needs, we have an opportunity to help a broader group of learners and workers advance in career pathways for employees' and employers' mutual benefit.

Reflections and Intentions

- Reflect on the last several weeks' worth of lessons you've facilitated. Did any of them connect to the SEL skills noted in this chapter, explicitly or implicitly? If implicitly, would you do anything differently after reading this chapter?
- How does your current course syllabus, state standards, or training program scope and sequence directly connect with SEL? If it doesn't, where can you introduce concepts without disrupting your overall agenda?
- Are there informal ways to bring the language of these two frameworks—or another of your choosing—into your work? What are two actions you can take in the following month to attempt this?

4 Does Teaching Social-Emotional Learning Work?

"In my mind, the purpose of education is to enable human beings to develop to their full potential, intellectually and spiritually. That means that students have to be empowered to pursue self-knowledge and the skills that will help them be of service to their fellow human beings. Education should encourage people to develop their curiosity about life; above all, it should not trivialize either the students or their lives."
—Michael N. Nagler

We have shared an understanding of what constitutes social and emotional learning (SEL). Now, we must highlight the effectiveness of teaching SEL. The investment of time, energy, and resources needed to teach SEL requires an answer to important questions: Does this work? What difference does it make to academic performance, student well-being, and employability? Are the effects, if any, short-lived or long-lasting?

These questions are essential as educators seeking additional resources to increase SEL education need top-level buy-in from their educational institution or training organization. Also, educators are sometimes tasked to build a case for integrating the teaching into the classroom's existing priorities (e.g., state standards for curriculum, or a packed technical skills agenda), whether it be with administrators, parents, or funders. This chapter will provide an evidence-based overview of recent research that presents valid and reliable answers to these questions.

The volume of studies investigating SEL is wide and deep. To get to the heart of the learnings and surface trends across the research, we'll dive into relevant meta-analyses. A meta-analysis is the result of a statistically driven process that synthesize the findings of multiple studies examining the same topic. This "meta" approach is widely regarded as the crème de la crème approach for arriving at a reliable and valid understanding of whether something works—in this case, SEL learning and teaching. For those familiar with educational research, you know that research studies often throw up contradictory evidence. This means there's a real danger of cherry-picking data to suit our biases and arguments. So, instead of highlighting one, or a small handful of studies, I'll share results from a range of meta-analyses that take a systematic approach to find an overall effect for specific questions. While no research approach is perfect—averaging can sometimes hide unique gems—meta-analyses give us a reliable answer as to whether SEL skills and their interventions work. I could continue sharing my own stories of witnessing SEL bringing personal and academic success to students, and I could share very positive feedback from students' families and employers over the past 20 years on their related experiences. Yet, it wouldn't be responsible of me to just share anecdotes when excellent scholarship exists to justify the work.

In this chapter, I'll share research that highlights a range of outcomes. I start by exploring the associative links between different social and emotional skills, specifically emotional intelligence (EI) and moral reasoning on academic performance. Then, I consider academic achievement from a different perspective: do school-wide SEL programs at various age levels lead to more extraordinary academic achievements? More specifically, I look at the relationships between SEL skills and academic performance and emotional well-being. Then I take a step back from outcomes to reveal what SEL inputs are most effective. In other words, what are the essential ingredients to deliver a successful SEL program? With this current stance, I then turn to the future—what is the effectiveness of SEL teaching both in the short term and the long term? Finally, as increased employability is the goal, I cover how SEL, in particular EI, is associated with job performance.

Let's get started.

Emotional Intelligence and Academic Achievement

Throughout this book, social-emotional skills are positioned as essential skills to leverage when increasing employability. This emphasis, however, should not mask the importance of academic achievement. To that end, let's start with academic performance because SEL "allows students to connect with others and learn in a more effective way, thereby increasing their chances of success both in school and later life" (Corcoran et al., 2018). Both "connecting with others" and "learning in a more effective way" are, undeniably, skills that benefit learners both in school/training environments and in workplace settings.

Before going further, it is important to note that *how* SEL enhances academic achievement is still debatable. Some theorists believe SEL competencies indirectly improve academic performance by creating a virtuous cycle—a self-supporting loop that uses inputs and feedback to continuously develop new learnings and skills. From this perspective, SEL improves attitudes toward school, self, and others, and boosts self-esteem and reduces problem behaviors and stress. Together, these enhancements collectively contribute to better academic performance. Alternatively, some think SEL competencies change teaching practices that, in turn, enable richer classroom cultures. This learning environment, in turn, increases academic engagement and performance, as grit, self-regulation, and attention are heightened. While we'd like to understand better *how* SEL works, this doesn't hold us back from asking the core question: do SEL competencies improve academic achievement?

Regarding EI, the answer is "yes." First, let's unpack the different ways scientists measure EI. First, there's the difference in *how* they measure EI, with most using ability or rating scales. Where ability scales are adopted, test-takers respond by demonstrating knowledge or processing emotion-related information. In contrast, rating scales are where learners report their level of agreement with a range of statements—for example, "I can handle most upsetting problems."

But EI measurements also differ in *what* they measure. This comes down to how a scientist or researcher theoretically understands EI. There are two prevalent theories for this—the mixed model and the ability model. As the name suggests, mixed EI covers a broad mix of concepts, including character, motivation, and emotion-related behaviors. In contrast, ability models understand EI as a cognitive ability like verbal or quantitative skills, except the focus involves emotions. Ability EI is often measured in four different ways, according to the four-branch model proposed by Mayer and Salovey (1997):

- perceiving emotions accurately
- using emotions to make decisions

- understanding emotion
- managing emotions

Given the difference between measurements and focus, the meta-analysis conducted by Corcoran et al. in 2018 investigated the links between EI and grades regarding ability EI, self-rated EI, and mixed EI. What did they find?

There is a small to moderate relationship between EI and academic performance. EI shows incremental validity over and above that explained by intelligence and personality, particularly for mixed EI, and understanding and managing emotions. However, while EI uniquely contributes to grades, traditional intelligence measures remain the strongest predictor of grades. Nonetheless, in terms of EI, ability EI was the strongest predictor of grades compared to mixed EI or self-ratings. Interestingly, compared to previous, outdated meta-analyses, there were no more substantial effects for younger learners. EI skills are important from elementary level up to university students. Most encouragingly, this was no difference in outcomes based on the proportion of ethnic minority students in classrooms. EI benefits everyone. These results show that while building traditional cognitive abilities are a must in education, so is building EI. Clearly, it's a win-win if EI is taught as an integral part of education alongside traditional skills.

Links between Moral Reasoning and Academic Performance

You will recall that social and emotional learning includes moral reasoning—that is, responsible decision-making. It's not hard to understate why this SEL competency is in high demand nowadays. Every day, endless headlines shine light on some type of personal or professional misconduct. Fraud, discrimination, and other crimes are ubiquitous. As a potent antidote, moral reasoning is an essential component of SEL. But is responsible decision-making linked with academic achievement?

It's worthwhile to articulate how moral reasoning was measured here as there is a dizzying array of measures. Corcoran et al. (2019) searched for studies that used the Defining Issues Test (DIT). This presents respondents with six hypothetical dilemmas, where respondents rank and rate different courses of action. Presenting specific dilemmas is a concrete measure, eliminating the broad personality type measures we often see. And while some dispute whether moral reasoning is any different from general intelligence, DIT research suggests that "moral judgment development as measured by the DIT provides a unique source of information that cannot be explained by general/verbal ability" (Corcoran et al., 2019). In terms of academic achievement, the 18 studies in this meta-analysis measured achievement in various ways, including GPA scores, the Kaufman Adolescent and Adult Intelligence Test, and several metrics.

Corcoran and her colleagues found a positive relationship between moral reasoning and academic ability regardless of how achievement is measured. Moreover, this meta-analysis stands out from previous research, as many studies overlook the range of factors that can moderate the link between moral reasoning and academic achievement. In this respect, Corcoran and her colleagues considered factors such as religiosity and personality. For example, religion, of any persuasion, held no influence over moral decision-making—not as an overall effect at any rate. Likewise, neither did personality show a significant relationship with moral reasoning.

Either way, educators and trainers can stand on the repeated findings that show that yes, moral reasoning is positively linked with academic achievement. This helps build the investment case for teaching and building SEL skills. But while we know that SEL is related to academic performance, what does the research say regarding school interventions?

School-Wide SEL Programming's Impact on Academic Performance

As an educator and, frankly, a human on Earth, you know someone can excel in one subject or discipline while struggling in another. Likewise, an SEL intervention may positively influence one academic domain but not another. And this is the crucial strength of the meta-analysis carried out by Corcoran et al. in 2018. Their meta-analysis is not only relatively recent and focuses exclusively on methodological rigor; it is also quite focused. Unlike previous meta-analyses (e.g., Durlak et al., 2011), their research teases apart the school-wide SEL contributions to reading, mathematics, and science among pre-K–12 students. Not only that, but their meta-analysis also sought to compare (1) the effectiveness of different types of interventions, (2) different subgroups (elementary and secondary), and investigated (3) the overall effect of social and emotional learning interventions.

Overall, the authors' meta-analysis found a positive effect for SEL interventions on reading and mathematics. They also found a smaller, yet still positive effect on science. Significantly, these effect sizes did depend on the type of intervention. For instance, *Positive Action* stood out, a six-unit curriculum taught in K–12 classrooms where intellectual, physical, emotional, and social areas are promoted. What's more, effects were greater where school-wide development programs, parent programs, community programs, and counselor programs were also in place. However, no effect was found to show whether SEL was more effective when taught at the elementary or secondary level; in other words, the education stage appears irrelevant. All told, SEL school-wide interventions do appear to impact academic performance across different subject areas positively. But this moderately positive result is likely to remain modest. Plenty of other influences—such as excellent teaching!—also contribute to academic performance. Still the evidence is compelling. SEL interventions can and do work. But what about older learners, and do the positive impacts go beyond academic performance?

School-Wide SEL Programming's beyond Academic Achievement

Academic achievement is crucial, but so is student well-being, navigating conflict, and knowing how to use and manage emotions effectively. Goldberg et al. (2019) analyzed 45 studies (30 interventions) involving 496,299 participants aged 4 to 18 years old. This latest analysis presents promising results for several outcomes: social, emotional, and behavioral adjustment; managing substance abuse; and reducing psychopathologies such as anxiety and depression. I should point out that this meta-analysis also studied academic achievement, yet while no effect was observed, their sample was too small (N=8) compared to the weighty study reviewed earlier.

The research indicates that a school-wide approach works across all ages. Post-intervention outcomes demonstrated small but significant improvements in social and emotional adjustment, behavioral adjustment, and internalizing symptoms (e.g., depression/anxiety). The most robust findings were for social and emotional adjustment. However, it's also worthwhile to mention that this, and other studies, consistently point to the importance of high-quality implementation—not all interventions are of the same quality. Excellent implementation demands a lot of planning and support. Not only that, delivering a high-quality program goes beyond an institution's walls; an excellent SEL program also involves parents and the local community. All this demands the right ethos, infrastructure, and effective partnerships. So, while this meta-analysis shows that SEL inventions do work, it also highlights how important quality is to deliver a good return on investment when teaching SEL.

These points beg the question: which program ingredients, in combination, are more likely to drive successful outcomes?

Characteristics of Successful SEL Programs

Despite the outcomes uncovered in the research, the truth is that some SEL programs work, and some don't. Research shows that individual SEL programs don't consistently achieve the impressive outcomes they were initially designed to deliver. So, while the meta-analyses mentioned earlier point to overall positive effects, the overall findings may hide the fact that some programs fail to get results. To uncover why this is the case, Wigelsworth et al. (2016) conducted a meta-analysis to evaluate specific factors associated with successful SEL programs aimed at students aged 4 to 18. These authors looked at three key factors: (1) the stage of evaluation, (2) the involvement of developers, and (3) the degree of cultural transferability.

The stage of evaluation—that is, efficacy versus effectiveness. Efficacy is gauged under controlled, ideal circumstances versus measuring the effectiveness of SEL interventions in real-world situations. Efficacy and effectiveness differ in two critical ways. First, the efficacy stage typically involves highly trained SEL professionals who supervise and coach implementation. This contrasts with real-world deployments, wherein SEL teaching staff often rely solely on their own expertise and often limited resources.

Secondly, while efficacy demonstrates the internal validity of a program before scaling up implementation, effectiveness determines whether the program is delivering its desired outcomes. You can see why there may be a gap between the efficacy and effectiveness stages. In real life, it's hard to replicate "ideal" circumstances. Worse, educators may not have access to trained SEL experts. Therefore, the Wigelsworth et al. (2016) meta-analysis investigates whether studies focusing on efficacy show more significant effects than those focusing on effectiveness.

The involvement of a program developer. Let's imagine a group has designed a specific SEL activity or program. Normally, this group would be involved at the efficacy stage—does their promised program live up to expectations? The program's developer and their customers both want to know this. However, as mentioned earlier, the efficacy stage is under "ideal" conditions. When it rolls out and scales across an entire school district or training organization, how effective does it remain?

On one hand, if the group that developed the program is involved in its initial evaluation, a conflict of interest could arise. This is known as the cynical view as bias may creep in. However, there is another take on this issue, known as the high-fidelity view. This perspective argues that if the program developer is involved, it will lead to better results. Why? Because they know the nuts and bolts of the program and have the expertise to guide its implementation. However, this too is problematic—if programs only work if program developers are involved, this has consequences for those who will one day implement programs on their own.

This meta-analysis sought to see whether a program developer's involvement shows a more significant effect than independently implemented programs. More specifically, they looked at differences between those programs that were led, involved, or independent of program developers.

The degree of cultural transferability. SEL programs have been implemented across the world. Does the culture in which SEL is implemented matter? How portable and adaptable are SEL programs if carried out in different countries? Most accept that some adaptation is needed to get a good match for cultural needs, values, diverse pedagogical approaches, etc. But if an SEL program is modified to meet specific needs, does this impact its expected effectiveness? This meta-analysis also sought to see whether implementation within its country of development origin (home) shows a more significant effect than those implemented in a different country (away).

This study measured a range of seven outcomes: (1) social-emotional competence (including social skills and interpersonal problem solving), (2) attitudes toward self (including self-esteem, self-concept, and general attitudes toward self), (3) pro-social behavior (including social awareness), (4) conduct problems (including anti-social behaviors such as bullying), (5) emotional distress, (6) academic attainment, and (7) emotional competence such as self-regulation. All in all, 89 studies were included in the study.

Except for social-emotional competencies, more significant effects were found under efficacy conditions. The rationale behind real-world implementation not faring as well could be attributed to program implementation that did not match the educational environment where the efficacy trials initially took place. But does this automatically mean we should aim for highest fidelity when implementing? If yes, this would likely require curtailing adaptations that are arguably important. Alternatively, my favored interpretation is that we should invest in more SEL training and a better understanding of what makes SEL teaching effective in the first place. This could swing the results back in favor of real-world implementations. After all, the results did show that real-world implementations can work better than efficacy trials when measuring social-emotional competencies.

Program developer involvement showed mixed results, potentially undermining the cynical view. Involvement is favored for pro-social behavior, academic achievement, and emotional competence, whereas independence produces more significant effects on social-emotional competence and conduct problems. As developer involvement was not enough to explain the differences between programs, something else is happening—an unknown factor. However, this discrepancy may be down to how involvement was measured. An SEL program is often lengthy, and a developer may be more involved at the earlier formative stage rather than the whole way through to summative results.

Findings also strongly suggest that higher fidelity programs produce better outcomes regarding social-emotional competence, attitudes toward self, pro-social behavior, and emotional distress. Worryingly, some programs made no impact at all when implemented in a different country from their origin. This doesn't mean to say they can't work. Instead, they simply didn't translate well to a different setting.

Adaptation is critical here. This is particularly the case as three outcomes did, in fact, fare better when "away" from their home origin.

This points to the need for "cultural tailoring"—we can't simply transport an SEL program from one context to another. We need to adapt and tailor while also making sure its core components retain essential fidelity. Trial and error are likely the best way to work out what to change and what to keep, to make a transported program work in a new context. It also matters who is at the table making the adaptions when transporting a program. Are similarly skilled SEL program developers from the destination country involved, or is adaptation left to local implementers—the teachers and trainers who oversee the delivery?

All told, this study provides considerable evidence that more significant effects are achieved when programs are delivered by external facilitators compared to teachers alone, but can still succeed if real-world implementers have the necessary confidence and skills to implement independently. Developer involvement also appears to help partly, but it is not enough to deliver the full range of outcomes.

In all, it's not just a matter of blindly implementing SEL to reap the desired benefits. We must select programs that are already proven to work; that is, they possess efficacy and are implemented (and adapted, if necessary) to suit a particular context. Adequate initial teacher training, ongoing coaching, and consistent implementation of such a program are also essential. But while a substantial number of interventions work as measured post-intervention, what are the follow-up effects? Are program effects still evident months, or even years, post-intervention?

Longevity of Impacts from SEL Interventions

Intervention results can be short-lived, regardless of whether we're talking about education outcomes, advertising goals, or personal life improvements, like quitting poor habits. Anyone responsible for the budget of an organization will be the first to ask: are SEL effects evident post-intervention months, even years, after an intervention is completed? This is the question posed by Taylor et al. (2017), who looked at the follow-up effects of school-based social and emotional learning interventions to promote positive youth development. Having reviewed

82 SEL interventions involving 97,406 students, they sought answers across a broad range of outcomes. These included the acquisition of social and emotional competencies, and positive and negative indicators of well-being. The results give cause for celebration.

The strenuous efforts of educators appear to pay off. First, all positive impacts were durable. Compared to student controls—those not exposed to SEL interventions—students demonstrated significant positive benefits across the board from 56 weeks and up to 195 weeks—3.75 years—since program participation. This is tremendous. What's more, a dual impact was observed; positive indicators of well-being increased, and negative indicators of well-being decreased. Notably, a protective factor was also identified. As we know, life has its ups and downs, and SEL interventions appear to buffer against life's problems. In other words, SEL interventions hold both promotional and preventive impacts.

As SEL interventions must be inclusive, it's heartening to see social and emotional gains regardless of race, socio-economic background, or school location. Also highly promising is the difference between post-intervention results and later follow-up assessments. Social and emotional competencies improved over time. This long-term adjustment, long after the intervention ends, is essential. Yet the results reveal that SEL skills, not attitudes, led to these positive long-term improvements. This doesn't mean that attitudes aren't important. It points to the pressing need to focus on skills development to leverage long-lasting change. As for long-lasting effects, some of the studies focused on the impact up to 936 weeks later, which is 18 years post-intervention. And this is where the results get really exciting. Small but significant effects were still found 18 years later. For instance, graduation rates and college attendance increased among those who had experienced SEL training in their younger years. Social relationships in later life also improved. Likewise, adverse outcomes such as arrests or clinical disorders were also less evident than controls.

This meta-analysis echoes the findings of a large longitudinal study conducted in the United Kingdom. While this study did not investigate SEL interventions as mentioned earlier, Goodman et al. (2015) looked at the effects of socio-emotional skills measured in childhood (aged 10) and their long-term effects in adult life. What they found points again to the long-lasting impacts of SEL skills. Those children with a high internal locus of control, good conduct, conscientiousness, cognitive ability, and sociability when young had measurable, positive impacts on their socio-economic status and labor market outcomes at age 42. For instance, those in a "top job" possessed more social and emotional competencies when they were young.

Given the preceding information, implementing interventions can lead to long-lasting results across many domains. Even better, the results get better over time. Those with SEL training keep using their skills. As an educator and lifelong learner, I am deeply encouraged by the findings present in the hundreds of studies tucked within these meta-analyses. Yet, while career success has had just passing mentions so far this chapter, I'll use this final section to highlight the links between EI and job performance.

Emotional Intelligence and Job Performance

None of us would be teaching or interested in SEL unless there were solid reasons for doing so. While the concept of EI has been around since the 1960s, Daniel Goleman seemingly popularized this term overnight with his 1995 best-selling book *Emotional Intelligence*. EI or EQ, for short, rapidly became a popular buzzword and has remained an intense research focus for social scientists ever since. Organizations left, right, and center also took note; EI remains a skill high on most employers' wish lists. This sustained interest in EI, therefore, puts the pressure squarely on educators and trainers to supply a socially and emotionally intelligent workforce.

A 2015 study by Joseph et al. shines light on whether EI links positively with job performance. You will recall that surveys often rely on self-ratings. This is a well-known problem as most people respond with a socially desirable answer—few want to paint a poor picture of themselves. Therefore, Dana Joseph and her colleagues sought a more definitive solution to this problem. Instead of relying on self-ratings of job performance, they conducted a meta-analytical study that strictly focused on job performance as rated by supervisors. You'll also remember that scientists measure EI in different ways, for example, ability and mixed EI. You've just read that ability EI proved a better predictor of academic performance than mixed. Yet while ability and more traditional skills are needed, mixed EI is broader in focus and, hence, a better match with the SEL skills covered in Chapter 3 (e.g., conscientiousness, emotional stability, self-efficacy, and cognitive ability). And this study is on point, as it included ability EI and a greater mix of SEL skills in the EI mix. So again, what did this study find?

This study gives us considerable confidence in the relationship between a broad mix of EI skills and job performance. Researchers found a significant association between mixed EI and job performance. There can be no doubt, therefore, why teaching SEL is essential. Not only have we established its links with student academic achievements and well-being, but the long-lasting impacts of SEL skills also improve employability.

The Case for SEL: A Summary

To make a logical, justifiable case for SEL investments, whether in the classroom, school-wide, or beyond, we must provide concrete evidence to win buy-in and resources. This chapter highlighted diverse and robust studies to provide such evidence. The meta-analyses highlighted can also offer considerations that can support you to improve the effectiveness of your implementation. It's best to select programs that are already proven; that is, they possess efficacy. Alternatively, suppose you discover a new, untested method or program that sounds potentially transformative. In this case, you could invite the program developer to conduct an efficacy study at your establishment—at their cost. After all, your establishment would provide the students and teachers; this also provides a great case study for the developer, not to mention a massive opportunity for your establishment.

None of this means you must invest in a fully fleshed out program in order to adopt SEL practices. I encourage you to take on what you can within your given context—even if it is just integration of small moments, at first. If you do want to make a case for organization-wide adoption, this research can help you demonstrate there is efficacy in these practices and can help you to bring others along if they need more substantiated evidence.

The findings also point to the need to network with other educators. Adaptability and fidelity are prominent themes, and they require a balancing act. By asking others for feedback, you can identify, for instance, whether their program of choice transported well to a context like yours. You'll also learn how much adaptation, if any, was needed.

There is much to be learned from those who have already done what we seek to achieve.

The next chapter details how to measure the effectiveness of your SEL programs. But first, I want to wrap up this chapter with another key finding. A study conducted by Belfield et al. (2015) looked at four different types of SEL programming to see if the interventions were financially successful in terms of a return on the investment it took to run the interventions. They found that the interventions were, indeed, quite successful, with programs consistently demonstrating financial value that outweighed the initial investment. In one instance, for example, a program called "Life Skills Training" or LST returned almost 20-to-1 on the initial investment. You may wonder what a "return on investment" can look like in an educational setting. What is measured depends on what matters most to the institution in the study and can range from tracking an increase or decrease in behavioral incidents, attendance trends, referrals to the social worker, academic performance, and more.

What interesting food for thought! What could your return on investment be, both financially and in terms of student success—emotionally, academically, and in terms of employability—both now and long into the future?

Reflections and Intentions

- If your teaching context includes structured SEL content, to what degree do these findings align with what you've observed?
- If your teaching context does not yet include SEL content, how has this chapter impacted your interest in adopting it yourself?
- What challenges would you expect if you requested SEL programming at your school, district, or training center?

5 Evaluating Social-Emotional Learning Needs, Activities, and Outcomes

"In all human affairs there are efforts, and there are results, and the strength of the effort is the measure of the result."
—James Allen

Getting buy-in and investment to implement social-emotional learning (SEL) is only part of the process. To implement and build SEL in students in both school-based and training settings, we also need to know how to measure and evaluate whether our activities are working. This is easier said than done.

Many potential pitfalls await when attempting to evaluate SEL implementation. First, there is no one-size-fits-all approach to measuring SEL effectiveness. However, there are better ways to go about evaluation, and it's important to know what's considered more robust and rigorous to gain meaningful insights. Further, comprehensive, and appropriate evaluation can be costly and ideally demands specialist knowledge. In this regard, I recommend bringing in the experts—whether that be in-house experts at SEL programs, academic researchers, or SEL evaluation consultants. If you do bring in external experts to support evaluation, it's important to know what's involved. This know-how will allow you to make the best choice in whom you select to help you evaluate your program. Therefore, I elaborate on best practices and how to benchmark, gauge, and evaluate the effectiveness of your specific activities.

The ideal scenario is to measure at different stages, from initial development to post-intervention effects. We'll consider three stages in this chapter:

- Formative Evaluation: the time spent preparing and planning for the program.
- Process Evaluation: the time spent during the program's implementation in real time.
- End-of-Program Evaluation: immediately after the program's completion and/or up to several years into the future.

Each stage involves specific questions, needs, and caveats, and it's helpful to know what each involves and how they work together to deliver a full evaluation cycle. Then, we'll consider certain issues that regularly arise within evaluation to help you avoid common mistakes. First—a closer look at formative evaluation.

Start with the End in Mind

Before we decide which SEL activities to implement, it's best to determine what form our SEL implementation will take. And what form our SEL training takes will depend on needs—what's feasible, appropriate, and acceptable.

For educators in a high school setting, for example, there are considerations around the age of students and whether certain activities will be deemed appropriate by both school and administration. There's also the pressing matter of academic standards and pressures for students to perform well on standardized tests, meaning prioritizing SEL activities over tested content may be hard to pull off.

For trainers who train young adults outside the K–12 setting, teachers may have more autonomy due to the age of the learners. Yet learner expectations could sow discontent if SEL activities are not framed well. They could feel anything that wasn't explicitly "hard skills" meant wasted time.

Some of these factors, and myriad others, are easier to manage than others when determining what form training will take.

To do this well, we first need to answer several questions.

- **Where is it needed?** For instance, if approaching from a district perspective, there may be differences between locations. One college offers different academic programs—if employability differs between programs, which deserves prioritization? Do nursing students need the same kind of SEL experiences as computer programmers?
- **What SEL skills are needed and why?** As already shown, there is a vast array of different SEL skills and frameworks. This question shouldn't simply probe which SEL skills are needed, but which ones need to be prioritized. This is best accomplished when the decision-makers have deep knowledge about various industries and what is needed to secure and thrive in employment.
- **Who needs SEL training and development?** Even with a school-wide approach, you'll likely break it down to the training needs for different grade levels or training cohorts as they are unlikely to receive the same training. Further, students' needs within a cohort will likely differ and may require different types of support. Hold space for the customization and tailoring that may be required for depending on the learner profile and program goals.
- **How will SEL teaching be provided?** As highlighted in Chapter 2, not all teaching approaches are alike. Therefore, will you adopt one developed program with proven efficacy, or will you pick and mix from several, or take a DIY approach? Will one instructor or trainer have dedicated time for SEL, or will this be integrated across sessions with all instructors and trainers? (I favor the integrated approach; however, I acknowledge there are constraints.)
- **How well will SEL teaching be accepted?** With so many ways to implement SEL teaching, which approach will be most acceptable for different learner cohorts? How familiar is your learner population (or cohort) with the broad concept of SEL?

- **How long will you run an SEL program?** This is important to ask. Consider this scenario: your organization has selected a program due to its documented evidence of success in bringing lasting change to learners. But it recommends a two-year implementation cycle, and your learners are only with you for a six-month boot camp style training experience.
- **How much will it cost?** You must also price your different options to find the best-case scenario for your school or organization. It is always wise to undertake a cost-benefit exercise. Ideally, you need to aim for maximum effect for the least cost. What is more expensive is not always better.
- **What do we care most about measuring—academic, well-being, or employability?** This most important question about desired impact provides the launch pad for the first step of formative evaluation: start with the outcome in mind.

What Does Formative Evaluation Involve?

It is easy to give these questions superficial consideration and quickly feel ready to launch the work. Yet, it's best to go beyond surface-level thinking to truly get ready for diving into the construction of your Formative Evaluation process. The following eight steps will structure your planning in a supportive and actionable way. Include decision-makers and critical stakeholders in the conversation as you and your organization work through them.

Eight Steps to Support the Formative Evaluation Process

Step 1: Determine the Desired SEL Outcomes

Before investing the time, effort, and resources into teaching SEL, it's essential to identify what is desired first.

And as educators, we know this all too well. We articulate expected learning outcomes as soon as possible: at the beginning of a school year or training cycle, at the launch of a new unit or module. The same applies to SEL. So, what are the desired outcomes of SEL training and development? We can ask this another way: "How will we know that the training worked?"

To do this well, make your outcomes SMART—specific, measurable, attainable, realistic, and time-bound. This time-tested approach to creating meaningful goals once again shines. Outcomes can be preventive or promotional in effect. For example:

- Program Goal: Reduce the number of reported behavioral problems by 30% by the end of academic year (preventive). Example Outcome Measure: School data—discipline incidence data.
- Program Goal: Increase graduate employability rate to 98% within the next three years (promotional). Example Outcome Measure: alumni graduate survey data.

Objectives are your steppingstones, but which objectives you choose will depend on the skills required to achieve outcomes, identified in Step 2.

Step 2: Align Desired SEL Outcomes with Learner Skills

There will likely be multiple social and emotional skills that are associated with each outcome you'd like your learners to achieve. This is where we identify and prioritize the desired critical SEL competencies to achieve the outcomes. For instance, emotional self-regulation would be a prime candidate for reported behavioral problems in a K–12 setting. In contrast, increasing the graduate employability rate of a training program would likely require a range of competencies, and those chosen should not only be relevant but also targeted—which Step 3 helps to achieve.

Step 3: Evaluate SEL Competencies

Once you've identified which SEL skills will best achieve desired outcomes, it's important to determine the extent to which these skills are currently possessed by your students. This will not only provide an essential baseline from which to evaluate progress and achievements (more on this later), but will also help you prioritize training needs.

(This is evermore the case if your program or school has the capacity—and/or expectation—that learning be customized and personalized for each learner). There are various ways you can create a baseline, or benchmark, evaluation. Prominent among these will be recording observations and undertaking surveys. The key steps here will be making sure your evaluations are both valid and accurate—again, more on this later. But for now, in terms of formative evaluation, it's important to know "where you are now" and which competencies should be prioritized.

Step 4: Determine Skill Gaps

Prioritizing skills means identifying where the gaps lie. For instance, if you were measuring "emotional self-regulation" along a scale from 1 (=low) to 5 (=high), and the average score was a 2.3, this would demand focused attention. It makes perfect sense to focus your precious resources on where the gaps lie, rather than taking a blanket approach. What's more, there will likely be variation among learners—which learners need the most help? If variation is high, this may point to the need to take a more tailored approach to targeting your training and development. I also recommend keeping an eye on whether your observations align with more objective measures. Take mental health. Some learners may cover up difficulties. Observations alone are unlikely to be enough to identify whether learners would benefit from relevant SEL skills. If both observations and survey results are aligned, this increases confidence in your baseline findings. If there's a mismatch, this requires deeper probing, like holding focus groups.

Step 5: Determine How to Implement Training

Once we know *who, what*, and *why* we want to teach SEL, we turn to the crucial question of *how* to teach SEL. Which approaches and activities should *you* select? Just as there are different frameworks for understanding and approaching SEL, there are different methodologies and activities we can adopt. We touched on some frameworks in Chapter 3 and have additional resources listed in the Resource Guide at the end of the book. Please note that my suggestions are also far from exhaustive—new activities and programs are fast arriving in the educational marketplace. Also, it is best if the programs and approaches closely align with your program's mission/vision, age-group, and learner profile. Also, capabilities, resources, and time are important factors. But as we pointed out in Chapter 4, so are efficacy and effectiveness.

You also need to figure out which teaching approaches would most appeal to your learners. Implementation is not just down to the content—we also need to factor in how the content will be delivered. Ideally, we want to mix things up—simulations, group-learning activities, role-playing, journaling, and so on; don't limit yourself to just implementing one approach to delivering content.

Also consider your context regarding online, in-person, or blended programming. A high school classroom with 20 learners in a circle will suit some activities much more than an online setting with 40 learners of varying ages joining from around the globe. What's more, these are teaching tactics, but we also need to determine how these fit in with our overall strategy.

There's a lot to consider at this formative stage, but this early evaluation would not be complete without costing our decisions.

Step 6: Conduct a Cost-Benefit Analysis

At this point, you've worked through five steps, and frankly, you may be looking at a big wish list. Simply put, it may not be possible to implement everything. Unfortunately, cost is always a constraint. It is imprudent to deny it.

First, weigh the costs and benefits from your wish list against your available budget; don't forget to account for the hidden, nontransactional costs of your time, and that of other educators and trainers. Think of the time they'll need to learn, prepare, and implement the chosen path. Thereafter, step back to decide what's in or out that can still deliver your desired outcomes.

This may involve some juggling and some patience. It may be that some activities or a particular program are just what you need, but you'll still need time to find the necessary resources to fund them – for example, identifying and applying for grants. Either way, it's important to know upfront what the expected investment is, and the return you are likely to reap, if your SEL activities are successful.

Step 7: Prioritize and Strategically Plan SEL Training Needs

Once the preceding six steps are complete, you are in a strong position to prioritize what, where, when, and whom you want to train. And importantly, you'll want to get in place a strategic plan to make this all happen. To place your SEL program of activities in the strongest position, ensure everyone's on board. You need widespread buy-in and a shared purpose, vision, and motivation to make it happen. List all possible stakeholders and share your list with peers to ensure it is comprehensive and strategic.

We're not finished yet. Step 8 is also needed *prior* to implementation.

Step 8: Plan for SEL Training Evaluation

The final formative step is working out, before you start, how you will determine whether and to what extent your SEL training is working. This is not limited to how effective your implemented activities are in terms of outcomes and long-term impact. You'll also want to know whether the form of your selected training best meets learners' needs and how well implementation is going. This will allow necessary adaptations and improvements. So, let's now turn our attention to process evaluation.

What Does Process Evaluation Involve?

Understanding whether your implementation processes are working in "real time" is hugely important. No one wants to find out at the program's end that it didn't work. Success is never guaranteed, and it's important to embrace learning from mistakes. As the saying goes: fail fast, succeed quicker.

There's yet another reason why process evaluation is so important. You will recall from the previous chapter that there's still a fair amount of debate about *how* SEL works. We know it works, but *what exactly* is giving rise to these impressive results? Knowing the "how" provides the necessary insight to make our programs better by doing more of what works and reducing or dropping what doesn't. It also increases our confidence in what we're doing.

So, to clear up this debate, we need to dig into the "black box" and discover which mechanisms are at work—what causes, or brings about, the desired results? Be cautious, though—it's unlikely to be one factor. Several things are likely happening. Even if that's so, it is good to know what it is about your SEL activities that will make a learner's face light up and say, "I get it!" or "This is really working!"

The overarching research questions you'll answer during your process evaluation could include the following:

- How are SEL activities being implemented? For instance, are activities being done with total fidelity or is there variability in their implementation, for example, differences between teachers?
- What challenges are often encountered during delivery? What lessons could be learned for improvement moving forward?
- What is ongoing monitoring data telling us? Are learners satisfied with the program? Are engagement levels high?
- Which activities are standout moments that contribute the most to satisfaction and engagement? Importantly, probe and reflect on why.
- Are teaching staff being sufficiently supported to deliver implementation well?

All these questions indicate that process evaluation is multi-stranded. Strands focus on specific activities and different questions related to constructive decision-making.

Exploring the Kirkpatrick Model

In terms of learner outcomes, there are various models. One such is the Kirkpatrick Model, which is used to evaluate training programs (Kirkpatrick, 2016). This model suggests we can evaluate: (1) Reaction, (2) Learning, (3) Behavior, and (4) Results. Key questions, investigated where relevant, will support your continued process evaluation.

Kirkpatrick's Level 1: Reaction

At every point of implementation, we can both observe and assess reactions within our students. You may want to keep an SEL diary to record your *own* reactions to learner reactions.

Questions to probe include:

- How are learners reacting to the presented tasks? Are their faces lighting up, looking intrigued? Confused? Possibly even disinterested?
- Are you receiving more requests for support than originally expected, or do learners have the right kind of information—in sufficient quantity—to make good progress?
- Are the training activities satisfying to learners? Which activities are working best, or least, and for whom?

Kirkpatrick's Level 2: Learning

For any educator, this level needs no introduction. Nonetheless, rather than test SEL learning at the end of an activity or program, it's good to gauge whether progress is being made *throughout* the initiative. How you do this depends on the activity. For instance, if role-playing is the activity, is learning evident within each run-through of the simulated experience? Or, in mock interviews, are learners getting the hang of what's being taught and improving incrementally within a session? For instance, are learners increasingly looking the "interviewer" in the eye and providing more confident answers as they progress?

Questions to probe include:

- What varied methods of assessment data are you gathering along the way to truly showcase the demonstration of desired skills?
- Are learners inviting and responding well to feedback?
- Have you observed steep learning curves for some content pieces that could benefit from further scaffolding, support, or an alternative approach?
- Are you using real-time learning assessments, such as class polls, and mini quizzes, to act as knowledge checkpoints? Are learners completing these assessments with vulnerability and clarity?

Kirkpatrick's Level 3: Behavior

Significant results will be evident by learners putting their learning into action. As educators, it's intrinsically rewarding to see our learners take what they learn and apply it to their lives—thus reaping the results of their learning. You will see emergent change via your observations, student conversations, and how they respond to more formal mechanisms, such as a process evaluation survey.

Questions to probe include:

- Are learners evolving in noticeable, if even subtle ways beyond the SEL learning experiences? Are they communicating with you or with each other in different ways?
- Are students bringing new topics, or new interpretations of topics, to bear in other sessions?
- Are learners receiving information differently, especially when it comes to the sharing of feedback?
- Are learners' families or loved ones noticing change of behavior, for the better, at home?

So far, my focus while discussing the Kirkpatrick Model has focused on learners. But a key part of process evaluation is to not limit evaluation to learners. The processes and experiences of teachers, parents, and other stakeholders must also be investigated with curiosity. The teacher's voice is of the utmost importance.

Questions to probe include:

- Is implementation going according to plan as expected for you? (How often, when, where, and how long?)
- If things aren't going according to plan, what can you do to get things back on track?
- Are activities working well, or could they be improved?
- Are sufficient resources in place to create a happy, engaged classroom?
- Are staff, community, and program development partners working well together?
- Are further resources required?
- What does best practice for these activities and this content look like to you? Is this happening? Why, or why not?

Kirkpatrick's Level 4: Results

Iterative results during process evaluation need to be continually fed back into implementation to keep your SEL program moving forward positively. Again, keeping a record and using reflection is essential for experiential learning. This record will also provide valuable insights to understand better how the program panned out overall.

What Does End-of-Program Evaluation Involve?

Imagine you've completed a two-year SEL program. Has it worked? Was it worth it? How do you know?

There are three kinds of evaluation you can undertake that, while similar, evaluate end results from differing perspectives. These evaluations are not only important to satisfy curiosity and gain intrinsic satisfaction that your hard work has paid off. They will also likely satisfy funders or stakeholders who require evidence of impact and outcomes as well as summative results. For K–12 and nonprofit settings, these could be basic requirements for reporting on grants. For other training situations, being able to market concrete results to potential students is a meaningful win that helps justify the commitment, and expense, of an SEL initiative to the organization.

These three kinds of evaluation are Impact, Outcome, and Summative Evaluation.

Impact Evaluation

Ideally, the right time to conduct an impact evaluation is right when your program ends or up to six months post-intervention. This will assess the immediate effects of your program and focuses on program objectives—the steppingstones that you identified during your formative evaluation.

Let's recall the two examples of desired SEL outcomes from Step 1. The preventive goal was "Reduce the number of reported behavioral problems by 30% by the end of the academic year." At the end of the year, then, it's time to run the reports. How many reported behavioral problems were captured in that final moment in time? Impact evaluation is appealing because its immediacy compared to program completion harnesses the enthusiasm and energy surrounding the program. If your SMART outcomes were drafted to require data that is easily gathered and applied, all the better.

The other goal example noted in Step 1 was the promotional goal: "Increase graduate employability rate to 98% within the next three years." You would measure the objectives established to reach this goal and evaluate, for example, the extent to which learner confidence in interview skills increased.

In brief, in this initial Impact Evaluation, we're looking at the immediate impact of your SEL program.

Outcome Evaluation

This post-intervention evaluation analyzes the long-term effects of your program. It has two key differentiators from impact evaluation. First, it's carried out at least six months after program completion and can be repeated over time to evaluate longer-term effects in a similar fashion to what we saw in the previous chapter. Second, outcome evaluation measures how well the SEL program goal(s) or desired outcomes have been achieved.

Here, we ask: has the overall SEL program goal been achieved? Which, if any, factors outside the program contributed to or hindered the desired change? What, if any, unintended change, for better or worse, occurred because of the program? The emphasis on outcomes doesn't mean to say we don't measure skills. Far from it. Measuring specific SEL skills at the same time as outcomes helps to identify which skills contributed to the success or not of the program. However, the key focus is on goal success—did the program produce long-lasting effects and achieve the goal(s)?

It can be challenging to acquire the inputs and data needed to have a robust and evidence-based Outcome Evaluation. This is particularly true for training settings that graduate small numbers of learners periodically, or for any school or organization that doesn't put budget against tracking alumni and learning from their post-program/graduation experiences. The difficulties in obtaining meaningful data should not, however, defer programs from attempting this style of evaluation.

Summative Evaluation

The third component of end-of-program evaluation focuses on practical matters and is a valuable exercise to undertake. Considering the whole program cycle from start to finish, the aim of Summative Evaluation is to leverage better decision-making. Questions probed in summative evaluation include: Do we continue the program? If yes, do we continue it entirely, or do we continue with some parts and drop or replace others? How sustainable—in terms of costs, time, and effort—is the program? Which program components helped or hindered the program? What recommendations have emerged out of the program?

Many among us have witnessed a successful initiative bring great impact to a school or training program, only to see it disappear after the successful pilot has concluded. A thorough Summative Evaluation can prevent that from happening at best, or at least clarify the rationale for discontinuation if such is unavoidable.

This leads us to an important factor that undergirds all three end-of-program evaluations. To make informed summative decisions and glean valuable impact and outcome evaluation results, you must consider the research design problem. That's because if the structure of our analysis doesn't meet best practices, the insights we gain are likely to be misleading.

Best Practices in Experimental Design

Unfortunately, it's not enough to measure SEL skills at the formative stage and repeat post-intervention at either impact or outcome stages, to assess the pre-post difference. Pre- versus Post-SEL program evaluation alone isn't robust enough to gain genuine insights as to whether our SEL program has worked well. That's because we can't know if any detected change is down to the program or other factors. Instead, we need to consider evaluation design and, more importantly, the need to take an experimental approach.

Consider the evaluation types noted in Figure 5.1, including what would be gained and lost in your comprehensive evaluation plan if a particular evaluation type was forgone.

True experimental and quasi-experimental research designs are the best approaches to evaluate whether an SEL program achieves its goals. The gold standard is a randomized controlled experiment, as this will provide a high level of confidence for the relationship between cause (your SEL program) and effect (the impact and outcomes). A true experiment will consider and control for all the critical factors that could affect SEL skill improvements.

Evaluation types	When to use	What it shows	Why it is useful
■ Formative Evaluation ■ Needs Assessment ■ Feasibility Analysis	■ Before/during the development of a new program ■ When an existing program is modified or transported to a new setting	■ Identifies whether the proposed SEL is needed, feasible, and acceptable ■ Evaluates the extent to which desired outcomes are possible	■ Allows for modifications to be made before full implementation starts ■ Maximizes the likelihood that the SEL program will achieve desired outcomes
■ Process Evaluation ■ Program Monitoring	■ When program implementation starts ■ During implementation	■ How well SEL program is working ■ Establishes the extent to which the program is being implemented as designed ■ Whether the program is accessible and satisfactory to its target learners	■ Provides early warning signs to any problems ■ Allows programs to gather and monitor feedback/results and adapt if necessary
■ Impact Evaluation	■ At end of program implementation	■ How well the program achieved objectives	■ Identifies whether established objectives program was successful
■ Outcome Evaluation	■ After a six-month interval post-intervention ■ Can be repeated over longer time periods	■ Evaluates how well the overall SEL goal(s) were achieved ■ Identifies whether effects were long-lasting	■ Provides evidence of SEL effectiveness ■ Informs policy and future funding decisions
■ Summative Evaluation	■ At end of program implementation, that is, post-intervention	■ Evaluates the summative results ■ Informs future program participation	■ Identifies what contributes to program success (or failure)

Figure 5.1: A summary of evaluation design types.

This ideal is often impossible or simply not practical. That's why quasi-experiments are usually undertaken. A quasi-experiment does not randomly assign learners to either a treatment (i.e., SEL intervention) or control group, nor does it attempt to state that the control and treatment groups are alike. Instead, it attempts to control for as many differences as possible statistically. Yet, while a quasi-experiment can mimic an experiment and offer a high degree of confidence in results without randomization, here's the rub. How do you choose a comparison group, a cohort of learners who will not receive the intervention? Often, we don't; leaving out some of our students is a step too far. If you are a trainer who trains one cohort at a time, not only would this be unkind, but it would be nearly impossible to implement.

I hear you. It is both logistically and morally undesirable to leave our learners out of an SEL intervention. We don't want to cause harm; if it doesn't go without saying, any SEL intervention should do its utmost to avoid causing harm to learners—socially, emotionally, or physically. Inclusiveness is important. So, what can we do if we can't or don't wish to take an experimental approach?

Even though this forces us to forgo demonstrating cause and effect by randomizing learners into treatment and control groups, we still have a few options. Some SEL programs already have national data sets against which we can compare our learner data. That's a pretty good measure of difference. Failing that, we keep to a pre- and post-SEL intervention design; however, we just make it as robust as possible! Our evaluation results won't be published in a peer-reviewed education journal. But that's not our aim. Instead, we need to make our measurements as valid, reliable, and meaningful as possible.

How Do We Robustly Measure SEL?

While it's beyond the scope of this book to dig into the nuts and bolts of measurement, I must draw attention to the primary considerations thereof, even if you're not personally responsible for measuring SEL skills. So, while it's more likely your education establishment will use an expert, whether the program developer, a consultant, or an academic, it's still important to know what robust measurement involves. Here, an overview of various important factors sheds light on how to generate credible insights into the effectiveness of your SEL activities. These can also be applied to any evaluation stage, from formative to impact. The first aspect to consider is the quality of measurement.

Validity and Reliability

When it comes to quantitative measures, we immediately think of numbers. But numerical measures are pointless unless they are valid and reliable. Validity means that a quantitative scale measures what it's designed to measure. Think of a car's speedometer. The whole point of a speedometer is that it measures speed. But what if there's a mistake, and you discover it's measuring the car's engine oil levels instead? This would make it an invalid measure of speed.

While this speed scenario is unlikely in the real world, it is more than possible when measuring SEL skills. So, the first important question is: Are your quantitative SEL measurements (e.g., survey instruments) measuring what you intend? Before I advise how to find and use such measures, we also need to discuss the other side of the coin—reliability.

Back to our speedometer metaphor. Imagine cruising along a rural highway at 60 mph, safely under the 65-mph speed limit. Suddenly, blue lights flash at you. The police pull you over; you're told you were driving 5 mph over the speed limit. This shows the difference between validity and reliability. Your speedometer is *valid*; it measures speed—just not accurately! Likewise, while a survey instrument may measure, let's say, moral responsibility, it may not be a trustworthy scale that gives *reliable* data. Therefore, if we want to determine if our hard efforts in teaching SEL skills are working, we must also ensure that our measurements are valid and reliable.

In the same way people sometimes underestimate the necessary training and expertise to teach well, we as teachers and trainers should not underestimate the expertise required to design a sound survey instrument. It's a science, art, and craft, and we best leave it to the experts. (I'd argue we each have enough to accomplish delivering our SEL interventions with skill and impact!) Nonetheless, we should always verify whether the offered scales have been statistically tested for both *validity* and *reliability*. As with many personality tests on the market, this may not be the case!

Thankfully, reputable scales will always publish their research findings. For instance, the Mayer-Salovey-Caruso Emotional Intelligence

Test Scale, MSCEIT for short, is the only commercially available emotional intelligence measure currently on the market; it is linked for you in the Resource Guide. It's also the most used emotional intelligence measure in academic research. Although there are several noncommercial alternatives, these tend to measure only one or two of the four branches of EI that were raised in Chapter 4. So going back to the formative evaluation stage, once we've identified the skills we want to teach, we also need to find reputable, fully tested scales to make effective evaluation possible.

While considering the quality of quantitative measures and data, beware of neglecting the trustworthiness of qualitative data. Quantitative measures are essential, but they are not the be-all and end-all. They only measure what they are designed to measure, so we risk missing surprising findings. What's more, if we want to open the "black box" and get a much better idea of how SEL works, qualitative data can provide rich sources of information. But that doesn't mean research rigor takes a back seat.

It means we do need to account for personal biases that may influence findings. We also need to acknowledge sampling bias and continually, critically reflect on the depth and relevance of our collected data. Throughout, we must meticulously keep records and leave a transparent trail of our data interpretations and decisions. We also need to attempt to find a comparison case, for example, another school or university undertaking the same program, and ensure different voices and perspectives are represented. Another point worth making is the need to record detailed, rich, verbatim descriptions of learner accounts. Quantitative results can be dry without the reinforcement of social proof and accounts. It's also a good idea to triangulate our qualitative data. In other words, don't rely on one source of qualitative data, for example, learner interviews. Focus groups, class observations, and open-ended survey questions provide rich, informative data to give us an ample sense of how our SEL teaching and learning are going.

Sampling

We can't end this conversation about measurement without mentioning the need for adequate sampling, if the burden of proof requires you to have an academic and deeply researched body of evidence (if not, you can read on as an FYI!). While randomization may be out of the question due to your class roster (aka, sample size), it doesn't mean sampling should be neglected. Some version of sampling is needed to caution against bias as it's easy to slip up even with a valid and reliable measure. When it comes to sampling bias, there are two issues we need to watch out for—self-selection bias (only those who want to participate opt in) and coverage bias (sample not representative of the population). There's an easy solution with survey instruments—make them part of the class activity so they are mandatory. That's the quick way to get a representative sample unless class attendance is low. Either way, always record the percentage of nonrespondents and check whether there's any significant difference between responders and nonresponders.

Here, I must draw attention to a likely occurrence—demographic data is usually collected alongside SEL measurements. After all, SEL outcomes need to be inclusive, and you'll want to link SEL findings to age, gender, and ethnicity.

Moreover, data needs to be linked to other relevant data, such as academic grades, attendance data, and so on. But while collecting representative data is relatively easy for survey instruments, this is not always the case with qualitative data. And in this respect, it's too easy to cherry-pick data unintentionally. If we only collect qualitative data from the most engaged learners, this can bias results in our favor. While this may help with the feel-good factor, we must ensure we listen to the voice of the least engaged. This will not only prevent bias, but will also provide fantastic insights to make our SEL activities as inclusive as possible. And responding to these data during implementation will lift our impact and outcome results across the board.

Ethics

My final point is the need to consider ethics. And for this, I would strongly recommend consulting your location's relevant research ethics guidelines. For instance, in the United States, we can draw on the Code of Ethics provided by the American Educational Research Association. With or without a guiding document or code of ethics to illuminate the situation, informed consent and anonymity are paramount—always. So too are sound data management practices to ensure learner data are secure and privacy is protected.

This chapter took us on a whirlwind tour of SEL program evaluation. While it's never too late to think about robust evaluation, it's ideally carried out throughout the SEL cycle, from inception to potentially years after implementation. And the more we integrate it alongside our teaching practices, the richer and more valuable the insights.

Moreover, mistakes are likely to happen—program implementation, particularly if you're new to teaching SEL, can be complicated. The road to success is sometimes bumpy, and your initial vision may not pan out as expected. But the more we keep an eye on processes and detach our personal preferences, feelings, and biases from the evaluation equation, the better positioned we are to catch and correct mistakes. In short, if done well, evaluation will increase the likelihood of making your SEL program a success, not just for you as an educator but for our learners and their future career prospects.

SPOTLIGHT STORY
The Chicago School Readiness Project

Early childhood interventions have long received both policy and research attention. The Chicago School Readiness Project (CSRP) was an intervention that received a best-in-class evaluation using several approaches I shared in this chapter.

What's the problem? Many children living below the poverty line in the United States experience higher rates of emotional, behavioral, and mental health issues throughout their lives. Similarly, children living in economically disadvantaged and often minority neighborhoods face major disparities in access to high-quality education. For instance, high school graduation rates among African American and Latino students lag woefully behind the national average (National Center for Education Statistics, 2021). These issues are not short-lived; the risk of detrimental effects stubbornly remains in later life.

The SEL objective? Early intervention is often the go-to solution to offset the devastating and inequitable outcomes we know that young kids continue to experience later in life. To help reverse these adverse outcomes, CSRP's intervention targeted Head Start centers found in high-poverty and high-crime neighborhoods in inner-city Chicago. Its core focus? To boost children's self-regulation and executive function skills by changing the classroom culture. Therefore, the intervention's objective focused primarily on targeting teacher's behavioral management strategies as the means to improve the children's own self-regulation.

The desired outcomes? By improving classroom practices and child self-regulation, the study hypothesized these changes would set children on "a higher achieving trajectory throughout school" (Watts et al., 2018).

Research study design? A cluster-randomized experimental design was used, where 18 Head Start centers participated. Centers were grouped into pairs based on 14 site-level characteristics, and each was subsequently randomly assigned to either a treatment (CSRP) or control ("business as usual"). The program ran two cohorts, with Cohort 1 participating in 2004–2005; and Cohort 2, the year later. Two classrooms per school participated, with a total number of 602 students.

The researchers collected baseline data at the start of the preschool year. Baseline data included: (1) a parental survey on the family and home environment; (2) direct assessments of children's cognitive, behavioral, and emotional functioning, and as per best practice, (3) observers also rated classroom environmental quality unaware as to whether the school was in the treatment or control group. These blind observations were also complemented by (4) teacher surveys on children's behavioral problems. Measures were again repeated the following spring to test for post-treatment impact.

To understand the long-term outcomes, study participants were followed into adolescence, with data collected during the 2015–2016 school year, that is, 11 years post-intervention for Cohort 1, and 10 years later for Cohort 2.

What were the findings? Given the research design, this study involved an array of eye-opening insights, which are highlighted below. These findings, published in several peer-reviewed scientific journals, are also summarized on the website of the Institute of Human Development and Social Change at New York University. These extensive findings are the results of a large team of researchers headed by Dr. C. Cybele Raver, a Professor of Applied Psychology (NYU Steinhardt, ND).

Increased readiness to tackle the challenges of elementary school. The CSRP intervention significantly increased preschool students' attention levels. Students also became less impulsive and increased executive function. Student academic abilities also improved in early verbal and math skills. What's more, Head Start teachers reported far fewer behavioral problems among preschoolers, who were happier and more social as a result. In brief, classrooms that focus on improving students' self-regulation help to reduce social and emotional problems.

Parents and families also benefited. The intervention didn't just help the preschoolers. Their families benefited, too. Moms of students in CSRP classrooms were far more likely to go back to school, with 27% completing a new degree. On average, moms of students in the intervention made, on average, $10,000 more a year!

Reduced teacher stress. Teaching is rewarding, but it can be a tough job. And stress can mount when we must deal with behavioral problems. So, it's great to see that findings reported that teachers were less stressed overall.

Mixed long-term outcomes. As previously mentioned, children were followed up around 10 years later. On a positive note, the evidence suggests that children in the intervention scored higher on adolescent executive functioning measures and academic achievement—clearly CSRP effects lasted into adolescence. However, not all effects were evident a decade later. Behavioral problems were insignificant. Surprisingly, maybe, those in the original treatment group, displayed "heightened sensitivity to angry and sad emotional stimuli." It would be good to see some more research to discover why this is the case.

Better later school selection. CSRP intervention students were also significantly more likely to be selected into higher performing schools, as elementary and middle test scores enabled high school enrollment.

All in all, these findings are impressive; using a high-efficacy SEL program works. But this spotlight also goes to show the benefits of a rigorous evaluation design; it offers an exemplar approach to designing and implementing a robust evaluation plan for your next SEL program implementation.

Reflections and Intentions

- Consider past innovations or programs you have delivered. How was that program evaluated? How does that evaluation compare to what's described in this chapter?
- Which aspects of a robust and comprehensive evaluation feel most inspiring? Most daunting?
- How does an evaluation plan benefit key stakeholders such as learners, instructors/trainers, administrators, district leaders, board members, funders, grantors? What does it require of them?

6 Overcoming Student-Specific Employability Challenges

"The greater the obstacle, the more glory in overcoming it."
—Molière

Throughout the process of developing this book, I had the pleasure of interviewing many educators who've helped countless students consider their career path. They shared stories about specific programs that promote critical thinking and planning next steps toward sustaining, satisfying work. Their experiences shed light on employability challenges and the strategies to overcome them that are outlined in this chapter. As mentioned earlier in the book, all too often, young people get the message that graduation and/or college admissions is the end game. So, what can we do to continue to promote employability skills and create environments ripe for fostering career ambitions?

The educators I interviewed often shared a common and quite straightforward response—that we should move away from posing the daunting question of "What do you want to be when you grow up?" Instead, we might consider other questions instead, like:

- What are your passions?
- What lights you up?
- What do you feel a pull or a longing for?

Additionally, how we can ensure that overcoming employability challenges is part and parcel of our everyday work? This includes and is not limited to:

- Exposure to careers.
- Igniting interests beyond those immediately accessible experiences.
- Increasing social capital.

- Strategies to overcome pressures.
- Building on students' strengths.
- Fostering a sense of belonging and confidence even in unfamiliar settings.

FROM THE PERSONAL ARCHIVE

Several years ago, I was a team leader for role-specific job training programs for young adults. I was touring a high school in Brooklyn, New York, and explaining our job-specific approach to curriculum design and program implementation. I named the programs that we supported (e.g., Junior Java Developer, Administrative Medical Assistant, Front Desk Agent). I explained how our program methodology focuses on the specific activities of a given job role, integrates technical skills with social-emotional skills, and provides the social supports needed to succeed on the job and beyond. The administrators of the school nodded and smiled and raved about how the methodology makes perfect sense and they understood why our results are so strong.

Then one administrator let out a big sigh and said, "But honestly, have you ever met an 18-year-old who knows what they want to do with their life? It's unrealistic to put them through a specific job-training program when they're going to change and grow so much."

They said it would be too risky to invest 12 weeks of a student's time when they might not follow through with that specific role because they are highly likely to change their mind about what they want. Everyone in the meeting vigorously nodded, and the path forward was clear—continue the status quo approach of delivering the standards-aligned curriculum and having students graduate.

For any student, no matter the age, the solution to not knowing what they want to do with their life isn't withholding information and opportunity from them or limiting exposure to varying options or unique pathways. Students bring their full selves to their classrooms every day. Whether we endeavor to engage their full selves is our choice and worth consideration. Considering their eventual, if not immediate, need to support themselves through paid employment, what are the steps that we can take, as educators, in helping students find their path?

Increasing Exposure and Igniting Interest

A colleague of mine taught middle school in Atlanta, Georgia, in the early 2000s. One day, she hosted a career day event. Instead of a traditional career day, where visiting professionals gave short speeches about their work, the eighth graders were tasked with igniting informal conversations with the visitors who were stationed around the room. The event was designed to mimic a real-life networking event.

One young man—we'll call him Marcus—approached one of the guests, an epidemiologist from a local research university. Upon learning that she was a scientist, he shared that his dream was to become a coroner.

"A coroner?" said the epidemiologist. "That's an interesting choice. How did you decide this was your goal?" Marcus shared that recently, his beloved grandmother had died in their family home. He had a vivid memory of the coroner coming to care for her remains, and he found out thereafter that she had died of kidney disease. He said he wanted to help find new cures for kidney disease so others wouldn't suffer like his grandmother did.

In an instant, everything made sense. He had a powerful and meaningful experience that impacted him deeply, and then he connected dots to the only professional person he'd seen involved in her passing. The epidemiologist tenderly described, as best she could, the work of a coroner. She also explained while he learned more about that role, he might want to look into becoming a research scientist or a medical professional. She didn't negate his interest in becoming a coroner but expanded his horizons by shining light on other options. Marcus left the conversation with the tiniest tear in the corner of his eye and the widest smile stretched across his face.

Exposure is important. You can't be interested in something you don't know about. The Future of Work is evolving fast; supporting learners to develop their own interests can prove a more motivating and enduring approach than building individual excitement around specific roles or careers that may change drastically before learners are ready to apply. How then can educators and trainers support a student's exposure to things that can ignite their passions?

Sparking student interest is a powerful way of overcoming a learner's frustration and anxiety about not knowing what they want to do

SPOTLIGHT STORY

Big Picture Learning (BPL) is a nonprofit organization that supports schools across the country. BPL began 27 years ago in Rhode Island and now supports over 80 schools in 28 states in the United States and many more internationally. They offer fellowships, internships, outside school learning opportunities and healthy living partnerships. I spent time with Casey Lamb, BPL's New York State Internship Pathways Director, to learn more about the nonprofit's work. One distinctive aspect of its approach is a student-centered and equity-centered method to identifying interests and learning from internships in rigorous ways. Their philosophies can be integrated into the classroom experience and are made stronger by the support of the classroom teacher.

With its partner schools, BPL works with teachers and classrooms to create space for relationships to be built. Advisory, or homeroom, is a space where this naturally happens. Casey described "Leaving to Learn"—field trip-like experiences where the focus is reflecting on experiences that sparked interest. The participants have gone everywhere from dive shops to yoga studios. Being exposed to and experiencing various opportunities creates space for learners to start reflecting and dreaming. Reflecting on what sparked their interest can help them consider what paths they might pursue in their future professional lives. The "Leave to Learn" experience is designed to give learners something to consider, rather than asking "What are you interested in" and waiting for the answer.

Classroom conversation, of course, is still a powerful strategy. Educators working with BPL love to ask: *What issues do you care about? When is the last time you felt really happy? Why?* Casey noted, "Teachers can then be the ones who help them to see the trends in their responses and name them. Is it doing something with their hands? Being in nature? Getting students into the world and reflecting on their interests can help them learn more about themselves and, in turn, have a better idea of what they like and do not like." It's one thing to have a good time during an experience. It's another to draw meaning from that good time and continue to develop ideas, dreams, and plans based on that meaning.

BPL is demonstrating that the teacher has incredible power to help name the learning that is happening through experiences. This is possible because the teachers know the students so well. They are incredibly positioned to join the reflections and discuss how it felt to "try on" certain experiences. Also, the teacher can support a shift in mindset with the collaborating internship supervisors, and business leaders can really appreciate all that high school students are capable of. Supporting universal career readiness at all stages of a student's life will show the world what students are capable of and, in turn, get students professional experiences early on. In case you needed another reminder, the influence of an educator never ends.

in the future. There are so many choices and so much fear of the unknown, and the path ahead is too often unclear and daunting. Other barriers—limited social capital and cultivating a sense of belonging include approaches to overcoming them.

Increasing Social Capital

If there was a simple, singular, silver bullet solution for breaking down barriers to career pathways, we'd already know about it, and we'd all be doing it. Yet the actual solution is multifaceted and continues to vex. New research has pointed to a rather important aspect: meaningful interactions among people who have diverse income levels. A *New York Times* article provided a layperson's summary of recent research by Raj Chetty and his colleagues (2022); their study noted that having more friendships between rich and poor was a key to reducing poverty. The core finding of the research, published in *Nature*, is encouraging: when people of diverse economic backgrounds develop meaningful relationships over time, the income gap between those people decreases (Chetty et al., 2022). In other words, while the financial circumstances into which you are born have strong predictive power over where your life takes you, an antidote is available—making friends with people whose circumstances are different from yours.

An obvious challenge to replicating this solution, beyond peoples' preconceived notions about each other, is the de facto segregation that exists in many of the country's cities and suburbs. Jessica Calarco, a sociologist at Indiana University who studies inequality in schools, notes, "Our society is structured in ways that discourage these kinds of cross-class friendships from happening, and many parents, often white, are making choices about where to live and what extracurricular to put their kids into that make these connections less likely to happen" ("Vast New Study Shows a Key to Reducing Poverty," 2022). Until children gain some independence as they progress through their teen years, young learners are less likely to encounter people who come from different financial background than they do unless their families create experiences for them where this is possible.

Discussing findings like these with learners requires much consideration; impact always trumps intent, and despite the best intentions, learners may feel targeted or singled out. Consider planning with peers and supervisors before facilitating open and supportive discussions about topics such as this.

Identifying and Overcoming Pressures

According to a 2021 JobList survey of over 1,000 parents and employed young people, 48% young people felt that their parents strongly influenced their career path, while almost 40% felt pressured to follow their parents' career advice ("The Impact of Parental Influence: Career Edition," 2021). Pressure from families and exposure to existing career pathways within one's family can be driving forces—sometimes positive, sometimes negative. This phenomenon, however, can often leave behind the specific skills, strengths, and talents of the individual student. Educators find themselves in an advocacy role; they may be directly influencing parents (e.g., through conversation, class communications, or report cards) in career-specific messages being sent to their children. In training settings beyond secondary education, opportunities to interact with your learners' families may be nonexistent, but the pressures could still be present.

The same survey identifies the rationale of the parental pressure, ranging from the promise of good future income to the belief it would bring happiness to the individual or prestige to the family. Educators understanding familial influences on students can influence families by sharing the student's talents, strengths, abilities, and interests and communicating the benefits of career pathways not yet considered that might be a good fit. Figure 6.1 shows top responses from JobList's survey.

In what ways did your parents influence or try to influence your career path?

- Discussed the importance of their career path
- Discussed benefits for the family
- Discussed benefits for themselves
- Their passion for their own job was inspiring
- Used guilt as an influencer

Why did parents push a certain career path?

Parent respondents who noted this response	Response	Employed young people respondents who noted this response
55.2%	Good future income	66.4%
28.1%	Pride in the chosen career path	45.0%
40%	Belief it would bring happiness	35.7%
37.6%	Preservation of family tradition	35.6%
27.1%	To achieve goals parents were unable to	33.2%

Figure 6.1: Survey results: rationale for parent influence on career decisions.
Source: The Impact of Parental Influence: Career Edition, 2021.

While influence on families is hard to enact, every teacher and trainer has the chance to influence learners themselves toward their own self-advocacy. A simple and powerful concept to combat this comes from *The Self-Driven Child* by William Stixrud and Ned Johnson, a parenting book published in 2018. The book's primary audience is parents seeking to do right in raising their children. However, the power of the concept holds true for teachers and trainers seeking to help individuals push back against societal and familial pressures. Like many impactful philosophies, it's elegant in its simplicity. "Start with the basics, by adopting the following three precepts when it comes to your kids: "You are the expert on you." "You have a brain in your head." "You want your life to work." When you buy into these three precepts, it's much easier to tell your kid, "It's your call." Sharing this philosophy with learners—and even with their families when given the opportunity—can have a lasting effect on an individual's self-actualization.

Powerful? Yes. Simple to adopt? Not always. It is a major mindset shift away from "parent (or other adult) knows best." It is a way of giving students power and honoring their thoughts, ideas, and voice, which can lead to much more fulfilling life paths down the line.

Identifying Student Strengths

As educators, we want to help students determine what they want to pursue and what is most aligned to their talents, strengths, and abilities. Short of having lengthy and repeated one-to-one conversations with each student—a logistical impossibility for many educational and training settings—where can we start?

Many practitioners use the Strengths Finder test by Gallup (or *CliftonStrengths test/StrengthsFinder 2.0*) as a good first step in giving language to students about their abilities. There is also a free test called HIGH5 (`https://high5test.com`) that can be a good starting place. I used to feel that some of these tests were inaccessible due to the cost or the recommendation to use an expensive, certified coach to guide you in interpreting the results. Now, I believe that teachers need to understand what tools are available to them based on the resources of their institution, while also understanding a test or tool's key components for themselves so that they can use the approach in their language with their students.

Additionally, there are many tools and resources aimed at helping young people pull out skills and strengths from existing experiences. Without support, many young people feel overwhelmed trying to compile their first résumé. Their perceived lack of professional experience feels insurmountable. But consider a young man who hasn't held jobs outside his home due to family obligations. His parents' work schedules have kept him at home every weeknight for his entire high school career. It was his responsibility to manage his younger siblings and their schoolwork, prepare their meals, maintain the household with regards to laundry and housekeeping, all while keeping up with his own studies and social life. This young man certainly has leadership skills, management skills, and personal responsibility in spades. Time spent coaching him on how to frame this on paper as well as during networking conversations and job interviews is time well spent.

Alternately, consider a young woman who likes to play around with computers for fun. She has hacked games, written her own scripts to accomplish simple tasks, and rebuilt computers using components she's sourced new and used from local and international vendors. She did this all in her bedroom with no supervision or guidance, save what she gleaned from online support groups and tech communities. A well-meaning adult may suggest she should have used that time to get a part-time job to earn money and "real skills." But clearly, she has built marketable skills based on an authentic interest—and the right coaching can help her follow this passion into a professional pursuit.

All young people spend their time doing *something*. They all like things and get excited by things. The more educators and trainers can help students acknowledge, understand, and harness their own strengths and interests, the more easily students can plan for and pursue fulfilling employment.

Cultivating a Sense of Belonging

Increasing exposure, increasing social capital, overcoming pressures, and identifying strengths can all work together to support a critical need among all young people—the need to feel as though they belong.

The feeling of not belonging is another barrier to employment for learners. I was recently reminded of this story when I interviewed Richard Bowden, the Head of the Career Center at De Montfort University in the United Kingdom. (De Montfort was featured in a Spotlight Story in Chapter 2.) Most of the students his program serves identify as coming from a low socio-economic background. He explained that when they send mailers outlining opportunities for internships within the community, the response rate was incredibly low. When he probed further as to why, the students told him, "I didn't think the mailer was meant for me" or "I do not belong in a fancy office building." Even when the student's name was printed in ink before the description of the opportunity, it still didn't feel real. It didn't feel like they belonged.

The sooner students feel a sense of belonging within and outside of the classroom, the more comfortable and confident they will be to reach out to new and promising experiences. After all, self-advocacy without a sense of belonging is a tall order for anyone—let alone someone new to professional settings. Teachers and trainers are critical members of a larger ecosystem that leaves learners feeling connected, empowered, and included. If learners have not yet felt a sense of belonging to the world of work, educators can support conversations, share success stories, and affirm students' journeys as they progress.

FROM THE PERSONAL ARCHIVE

I remember my first day of eighth grade like it was yesterday. Just shy of 13 years old, I arrived at my new school to be greeted by the fanciest lineup of cars I had ever seen (all driven by teenagers!), beautifully manicured lawns, and soaring brick buildings with majestic white pillars. None of this felt like school to me. I was a stranger in a strange land.

A few weeks prior, my family learned that I'd come off the waiting list of a prestigious private school outside of Pittsburgh. They were thrilled. Me? I was happy at my public school and did not in any way want to make this transition. I loved my school and had no reason to believe that I wasn't receiving a high-quality education. But my sister, who I'd later come to call my education advocate, was five years older than me. She didn't feel the high school I'd be attending was strong enough or would offer the opportunities she wanted for me. Attending the private school was a big sacrifice for my family—one only made possible through scholarships and loans.

Upon entering my first classroom, I overheard one classmate talking about vacationing in the Caribbean and another listing the classic books they read over the summer—all titles brand-new to me. One message reverberated in my head that day and for months to come: "I do not belong here." It was a different universe, one where I would never fit in and was not worthy.

I cried. A lot. My grades dropped significantly from the straight A's I was used to. I spent hours studying, and it didn't even seem like it mattered. My test anxiety caused me to go blank when it came time for a quiz or assessment. I would make some attempts to fit in, but I didn't have the life experiences or language to pull from that I felt mattered most with my new peers.

Like most things, it got better with time. I formed bonds with friends and found supportive teachers who identified my needs and helped me to—eventually—get good grades again. I started to gain more confidence and, even in a small way, I began to feel more of a sense of belonging. The famous words of Mother Teresa meant more than I'd ever expected. "The biggest disease today is not leprosy or tuberculosis but rather the feeling of not belonging."

Of course, I was lucky to attend this school. Regardless of how we paid for it, having access to this school offered me incredible privilege, and I remain grateful for the educational opportunity. Yet, it was nearly an experience of total failure that could have completely derailed my trajectory. Had I not found my way to a sense of belonging, perseverance, and self-awareness, helped in no small part by incredible educators, family, and a few dear friends, I would have experienced a type of failure that I'm not sure I could have come back from. I think of this often when I encounter young people who feel detached, unwelcome, or excluded from the world of work that awaits them.

Challenges beyond the Educator's Reach

Increasing exposure, focusing on strengths, increasing social capital, connecting to experiences to meet their goals, increasing a sense of belonging, and overcoming pressures—these are all powerful levers educators can use to improve employability for their students. Yet, there will be student-specific barriers that require the support of doctors, learning specialists, social workers, counselors, mental health professionals, or more. It is not possible or at all reasonable for educators to meet the full needs of their students, no matter their age or circumstances.

Potential barriers can include and are not limited to physical health; substance abuse; mental health; domestic violence; sexual abuse; low self-esteem; caring for children, dependents, or other family members; unstable housing; financial needs; and learning disabilities—diagnosed or otherwise. These are not to be overlooked or underestimated. Students with these needs deserve professionals who are expert in meeting such challenges. Making a support or care plan that is integrated with a student's hopes and dreams is possible, though even the act of making such a plan may be well beyond the duty of an educator. We may wish to solve everyone's issues, but that doesn't mean we can. And that's okay.

It is important that we as educators, as much as we are able, endeavor to "see around the corners" and potentially identify barriers and help facilitate ways to alleviate them. Whatever a learner's unique challenge may be, it will almost certainly be more easily supported if the learner—as an adult—has stable, fulfilling work that provides for their financial needs.

Reflections and Intentions

- Think of a specific learner you're currently supporting directly or indirectly. What are the strongest influences (positive and negative) driving their thinking about their future?
- Do you know if you have students who do not feel like they belong? If yes, what can you do to support them? If no, what can you do to find out?
- How can social capital be increased within a school or training community?

7 Establishing Common Language for an Employability-Driven Classroom Culture

"Nothing in life is to be feared, it is only to be understood. Now is the time to understand more, so that we may fear less."

—*Marie Curie*

Once, a high school teacher shared with me a story about one of her high-performing students. The young lady worked at a fast-food restaurant as her part-time job outside of school. She moved up the ranks quickly and was soon tasked with training the new joiners in addition to increased responsibilities around the store. The new teammates would shadow her, and she would teach them the standard operating procedures and best practices in completing the work.

That same student later applied to an internship that required an interview, after which she spoke with her teacher. She was feeling quite low. "They asked me, 'How have you demonstrated leadership skills?' I didn't know what to say." She felt leadership meant being the captain of the basketball team or the student council president; it certainly didn't apply to regular teens like her. When the teacher helped her reframe—for herself first, and then others—how her work experience demonstrated tremendous leadership, it was as if she saw herself in a mirror for the first time.

Educators and trainers can have meaningful influence over whether their own students face moments like this in their path to employment. In this case, the community of learners and instructors needs to share common understandings and language around leadership and create opportunities to discuss outside leadership experiences *inside and outside* the classroom. Students need repeated, intentional experiences designed to develop self-reflection skills, adaptive communication skills, knowledge of employers' needs, and self-confidence to articulate their experiences and value to others.

This may feel like a tall order. The constraints of budget, knowledge, and will can be hard to overcome, as is the often most prevalent constraint of them all—time. Vocational training programs target a specific skills agenda and may not have time on the calendar for additional content. In some instances, government regulatory boards may oversee the curriculum of a training program and specifically forbid adapting it in any way. The pressure put on public educators to deliver results on standardized tests can have a similar effect.

Common Language for Career-Focused Competencies

When schools and organizations start with a common language to describe desirable employability traits, they lay the groundwork on which workforce conversations and practice activities can build. If an organization does not have a unified understanding of core competencies that drive employability, this task falls to the individual teacher to define and apply the concepts. While going solo and doing this on your own isn't ideal, there are many frameworks and resources from which to draw.

Consider the work of the National Association of Colleges and Employers (NACE), a professional association for recruiters and college career service professionals. For nearly 70 years, NACE has been a go-to resource for information and insights on job market hiring trends, salary benchmarking, recruiting and hiring practices, and outcomes for graduates. Not surprisingly, it includes leadership in its "Competencies for a Career Ready Workforce Definitions." The association defines *leadership* as the ability to "recognize and capitalize on personal and team strengths to achieve organizational goals."

Imagine if the student in the preceding story had encountered this definition repeatedly, for a variety of purposes in a variety of settings—including those designed to support her as she pursued jobs and internships. She likely would have been ready with an authentic and appealing answer to her interviewer's question.

NACE notes eight competencies for career readiness as shown in Figure 7.1. Its website is also a community gathering place for teachers

Competencies for a Career-Ready Workforce as Defined by the National Association of Colleges and Employers	
Career and Self-Development	Proactively develop oneself and one's career through continual personal and professional learning, awareness of one's strengths and weaknesses, navigation of career opportunities, and networking to build relationships within and outside one's organization
Communication	Clearly and effectively exchange information, ideas, facts, and perspectives with persons inside and outside of an organization
Critical Thinking	Identify and respond to needs based on an understanding of situational context and logical analysis of relevant information
Equity and Inclusion	Demonstrate the awareness, attitude, knowledge, and skill required to equitably engage and include people from different local and global cultures. Engage in anti-racist practices that actively challenge the systems, structures, and policies of racism
Leadership	Recognize and capitalize on personal and team strengths to achieve organizational goals
Professionalism	Knowing work environments differ greatly, understand and demonstrate effective work habits, and act in the interest of the larger community and workplace
Teamwork	Build and maintain collaborative relationships to work effectively toward common goals, while appreciating diverse viewpoints and sharing responsibilities.
Technology	Understand and leverage technologies ethically to enhance efficiencies, complete tasks, and accomplish goals.

Figure 7.1: NACE's competencies for a career-ready workforce: definitions.

who upload strategies and tools to make these competencies come to life in their classrooms; the site is listed for you in the Resource Guide. When educators benefit from a common language, they can encourage and support each other's practice in explicit ways related to job-readiness.

Returning to leadership, NACE offers sample behaviors to flesh out its definition of this competency.

NACE Sample Behaviors for Leadership

- Inspire, persuade, and motivate self and others under a shared vision.
- Seek out and leverage diverse resources and feedback from others to inform direction.
- Use innovative thinking to go beyond traditional methods.
- Serve as a role model to others by approaching tasks with confidence and a positive attitude.
- Motivate and inspire others by encouraging them and by building mutual trust.
- Plan, initiate, manage, complete, and evaluate projects.

Start with a common definition, and then work to name skills, actions, and dispositions that make this definition come to life. If you have time in your course or program to do this collaboratively with students, great! If not, using an existing framework or set of definitions like that provided by NACE offers a great foundation. Work the definitions and sample behaviors directly into your classroom's culture via group assignments, peer-to-peer conversation prompts, personal reflections, teacher-to-learner coaching moments, and more.

To avoid the situation described at the start of the chapter, we must bring these career-focused competencies and real-life situations within our walls and, if we teach remotely, our Zoom rooms. This can be accomplished through micro moments and routines that will help enhance your learners' career journeys and decrease the disconnectedness between our classrooms and the world of work.

Before digging into more ideas and strategies, take a moment to reflect on the culture, strategies, and approaches within your own classroom that are setting up students for success in their eventual careers. Celebrate those moments! And now, let's add to your toolkit.

Common Language for a Culture of Learning and Teaching

I have observed classrooms with pre-kindergarten kids, mid-career switchers, and everyone in between. I have supported instructors on six continents. I've leaned into employability focused courses delivered in high schools, colleges, employer settings, and workforce development training centers. I am beyond grateful for the comprehensive exposure my career has granted me, especially as I can share with confidence an essential truth about the craft of teaching.

The principles of high-quality teaching and learning, and the discrete actions and activities that support the work, remain relatively consistent across learning experiences seeking to prepare students for career success. Given the speed at which the jobs landscape is changing, this consistency offers hope. Because excellence in teaching and learning is already consistent across disparate settings now, we can rest assured it will remain relevant despite the fast-approaching and unpredictable changes to the world of work. To ground us in the basics, let's look at some core tenets of teaching and learning that yield strong learner outcomes.

At my current organization, Generation, our training programs are short and intensive, lasting 4–16 weeks, usually full time. We serve learners ages 18-plus across a variety of countries. Our definition of strong teaching and learning supports our specific context—adult learners who are expressly interested in a new career. Country cultures, specific learner profiles, and learning setting (online, in-person, or blended) change from program to program, but the core work of training and placing learners into jobs does not. We support instructors through direct training, observations, and coaching to maintain consistently strong teaching and learning experiences.

Our Global Director of Instruction, Shalini Dwivedi, directs the ideation, creation, and implementation of our network-wide instructional strategy. In 2021, she led our organization through a rigorous process of surveying and interviewing teachers, coaches, alumni, and current learners to determine what qualities make an ideal learning environment. These actions are suitable for in-person or online synchronous instruction.

The purpose of this work was to clearly name actions and attributes that lead to a strong "Culture of Learning and Teaching." In the same way NACE first defined a core competency and then provided sample behaviors to make it come to life, Shalini sought to do the same with Generation's global understanding of excellence in learning and teaching. Figures 7.2, 7.3 and 7.4 share selected highlights from the culmination of her exploration, naming overarching competencies, defining characteristics and evidence-based behaviors that show how this looks and feels in a thriving classroom.

Again, the overarching competencies, the defining characteristics, and the evidence-based behaviors were synthesized from the inputs of hundreds of stakeholders: instructors, learners, program leaders, alumni, mentors. This common language was a true group effort and reflects the aspirations of the network. If these behaviors are present within any Generation classroom, we can be assured that excellent learning and teaching are in place that will lead to enhanced employability upon graduation.

Figures 7.5 shows a partial sample of a rubric developed to task teachers, mentors, and coaches with evaluating how well the aspects of career readiness have taken root for the learners. Because the rubric is used for coaching conversations between coaches and instructors, it is written in learner-focused language. Focusing on learner actions in the classroom sharpens the focus on learners, reinforcing the concept that learners' actions rather than teachers' actions are better indicators of classoom success.

The heart of employability lies in more than reciting technical knowledge and facts. The rubric, of course, captures the class's ability to talk about what classmates are learning and demonstrate role-based technical skills. It also captures the less tangible but equally valuable behavioral skills and mindsets—the terms Generation uses to describe the Durable Skills and SEL content discussed in Chapter 3. By drawing attention to notions of relevance and connections, it drives the instructor and the learners toward something important: a more authentic and enduring understanding of what they are learning as it relates to their real lives beyond the classroom.

Any rubric or tool that aims to qualify and quantify something this complex faces challenges.

Culture of Learning 1/2		
Active Engagement	Maintaining high academic expectations	■ Reinforcing shared and agreed upon academic norms when required and appreciating instances when learners met academic expectations ■ Maintaining the same expectations for all participants but differentiating instruction (e.g., using various forms of interface/multimedia, different assignment goals) to suit participant learning styles ■ Requiring learners to cite evidence to support their thinking or give rationale to support their responses ■ Letting no incorrect response slide by and providing immediate feedback or asking follow-up questions to clarify misunderstood content ■ Providing space for learners to clarify or ask follow-up questions from instructor or peers ■ Providing additional and challenging learning opportunities to learners who ask for it or are ready for it ■ Leveraging async learning data to clarify potential misunderstandings
	Building higher-order thinking skills	■ Utilizing a variety of facilitation tips to sustainably engage learners throughout the session ■ Asking higher-order thinking questions or facilitating higher-order activities and pushing learners to do majority of the thinking ■ Providing support necessary for learners to complete instructional tasks requiring higher-order thinking skills as independently as possible (e.g., scaffolding follow-up questions, facilitating peer support, utilizing wait time) ■ Providing opportunities within sessions for peers to engage in higher-order discussions and/or learn from each other ■ Demonstrating compassion toward learners of all learning styles and levels by encouraging all responses, accurate or inaccurate ■ Creating spaces for learners to lead learning wherever possible

Figure 7.2: Culture of learning core behaviors. The organization is Generation: You Employed.

Culture of Learning 2/2		
Peer Learning	Facilitating community-driven learning and growth	■ Personalizing sessions to incorporate spaces for peers to collaborate with each other and provide feedback when necessary ■ Providing feedback for both strengths and areas of development in an adult appropriate way ■ Creating spaces and systems for peers to support each other's growth both in and out of sessions ■ Encouraging learners to leverage additional support structures (e.g., office hours, mentorship sessions, peer coaching)
Self-Learning	Organizing learning resources and pathways	■ Collecting and analyzing learning data at regular intervals ■ Organizing resources for easy accessibility for learners and staff ■ Leveraging async data to provide differentiated and personalized support (e.g., office hours by themes or learning levels, extra sessions for select learners)
	Building life-long learning skills	■ Appreciating learner efforts as opposed to outcomes to encourage a growth mindset ■ Supporting learners in taking more ownership of their own learning journey (e.g., facilitating support from mentor or coaching them through challenges)
Instructional Time	Maximizing instructional time	■ Providing clear and concise directions often and in various ways (e.g., on a slide, voicing it over, copy pasting it in chat box) ■ Setting up and using efficient routines and procedures (e.g., set procedure for transitioning to breakout groups) and encouraging learners to show ownership of them ■ Prioritizing key content and activities in case of time shortage and managing time effectively during a session ■ Dealing with all technological issues and other unseen challenges in a swift and calm manner without losing out on instructional time, even proactively creating contingency plans for common challenges

Figure 7.2: Culture of learning core behaviors. The organization is Generation: You Employed.

Culture of Belonging 1/2		
Equity & Inclusion	Building a safe and supportive learning environment	■ Demonstrating and modelling respect, empathy, trust, and patience during learner interactions and in facilitating activities (e.g., respecting each learner's individual journey and, hence, understanding if a participant may be struggling at home and not reprimand them for not answering a question) ■ Creating spaces within and outside sessions to foster a culture of acknowledging and appreciating progress ■ Encouraging and appreciating interactions that are judgment-free (e.g., encouraging learners to engage fully and respond even if the answer may not be accurate)
	Creating a culture of inclusion	■ Reflecting on individual biases and judgments, and working to unlearn them ■ Continuously educating yourself on how to create an inclusive learning environment ■ Constantly reiterating the importance of creating a culture of inclusion and supporting learners to be shared owners of this culture ■ Facilitating spaces so learners get to know each other on a personal level and can be proud to share their identity markers ■ Modelling a culture of inclusion by personalizing session plans to make them as inclusive as possible, using inclusive language, leveraging experience that each learner brings, respecting cultural diversity and learning preferences (especially for neurodivergent learners)
Cohort Culture	Co-creating shared culture with learners	■ Co-designing norms and culture statements, aligned to culture of inclusion and professionalism, with learners to create a learning environment for all to thrive in ■ Reiterating norms and culture statements strategically to ensure they are upheld for duration of cohort
	Facilitating sense of ownership of culture	■ Creating spaces and structures for learners to take ownership of cohort norms and culture ■ Appreciating examples of upholding norms and debriefing nonexamples collectively to course correct

Figure 7.3: Culture of belonging core behaviors. The organization is Generation: You Employed.

Culture of Belonging 2/2		
Relationships & Support	Building authentic relationships	■ Creating spaces within and outside sessions for peers and instructors to build authentic relationships with each other ■ Leveraging relationships to support learners' growth by pushing them out of their comfort zone and supporting them through challenges
	Building a culture of respect and support	■ Demonstrating and modelling respect, empathy, trust, and patience during learner interactions and in facilitating activities (e.g., respecting each learner's individual journey and, hence, understanding if a participant may be struggling at home and not reprimand them for not answering a question) ■ Encouraging learners to support each other's growth and celebrating collective growth
	Facilitating community-driven learning and growth	■ Personalizing sessions to incorporate spaces for peers to collaborate with each other and provide feedback when necessary ■ Providing feedback for both strengths and areas of development in an adult appropriate way ■ Creating spaces and systems for peers to support each other's growth both in and out of sessions ■ Encouraging learners to leverage additional support structures (e.g., office hours, mentorship sessions, peer coaching)

Figure 7.3: Culture of belonging core behaviors. The organization is Generation: You Employed.

Career Readiness 1/3		
Objectives' Importance	Facilitating effective session plans	■ Clearly articulating session objectives and their importance, and referencing them strategically throughout the session ■ Connecting relevance of objectives to job and future career ■ Encouraging learners to make connections between session objectives and importance for potential future opportunities
	Gathering learning data	■ Checking for understanding throughout the session to determine whether learners can articulate the session objectives, their importance, and their connection to career ■ Strategically asking a range of open and closed questions to proactively gauge learner understanding around session objectives
Content Mastery	Preparing and personalizing session plans	■ Allocating enough time to ensure critical key points in a session will be covered ■ Proactively adding probing questions to uncover potential learner misunderstandings ■ Including any additional prerequisites required for the session based on learner demographics and learning levels ■ Including additional checks for understanding at strategic parts of the session ■ Leveraging async data to add clarification of misunderstood key points ■ Adding updated industry content and/or relevant real-world examples and experiences ■ Adding spaces for learners to engage in deeper and higher-order discussions
	Facilitating learning of content	■ Introducing and recapping key points throughout the session in clear and coherent ways, often using different mediums (e.g., on slide, voicing over) ■ Following the flow of the session plan, potentially breaking content into bite-sized chunks for better retention, to achieve session objectives ■ Delivering content in an engaging and confident tone

Figure 7.4: Career readiness. The organization is Generation: You Employed.

Career Readiness 2/3		
Content Mastery (cont.)	Gathering learning data	■ Checking for understanding (CFU) at strategic parts of the session via various modes, like during direct instruction of a complex topic, introduction of a new key point, before independent practice, and at a transition point through polls, chats, quick activities, or discussions ■ Administering end-of-session assessment or exit tickets to gauge session or content mastery ■ Strategically asking a range of open and closed questions to proactively address participant misunderstanding
	Responding to learning data	■ Asking follow-up questions to understand the root cause of learner misunderstanding and strategically spending time re-teaching or re-framing content to address the underlying root causes ■ Letting no incorrect response slide by, and providing timely and constructive feedback or asking follow-up questions to clarify misunderstood content ■ Leveraging async learning data to clarify potential misunderstandings ■ Supporting learners who arrive at the right answer by themselves or with support from peers as much as possible ■ Clarifying learners' misunderstanding before moving on to the next section

Figure 7.4: Career readiness. The organization is Generation: You Employed.

Career Readiness 3/3		
Behavioral Skills & Mindsets (BSMs)	Maintaining high professional standards	■ Clearly articulating and modeling professionalism as required by the industry ■ Appreciating examples of upholding professionalism and debriefing nonexamples collectively to course correct
	Integrating and modeling BSMs	■ Internalizing and modeling the relevant BSMs throughout the cohort ■ Posing higher-order thinking questions so learners can independently connect technical skills to behavioral skills and mindsets ■ Regularly reinforcing importance of behavioral skills and mindsets and their importance on the job ■ Creating spaces for learners to reflect on and plan their own BSM growth ■ Appreciating learner growth and instances of BSM demonstrations
Relevance & Connections	Connecting content to real-world examples and experiences	■ Sharing relevant real-world examples at strategic points followed by reflection questions to push higher-order learning ■ Creating spaces for learners to share own relevant real-world examples and experiences
	Connecting content to relevance and impact in career	■ Strategically connecting content or skills to its importance on the job and facilitating learners to do the same ■ Supporting learners in reflecting how learned content will have an impact beyond their first job post-graduation ■ Encouraging learners to connect current content with past topics or sessions to create a more holistic understanding of the role and improve their learning outcomes

Figure 7.4: Career readiness. The organization is Generation: You Employed.

Career Readiness 1/2

	Emergent	Foundational	Advanced	Mastery
Objectives Importance	Few learners can articulate the objectives of the session	Some learners can articulate the objectives of the session AND Why it is important for them to master it	Most learners can articulate the objectives of the session, why it is important for them to master it AND How it is relevant to their career	All learners meet descriptors for level 3 AND Ask questions beyond the session objectives to know more about future opportunities and careers in the field
Content Mastery	Few learners can demonstrate mastery over session/topic objectives by applying new skills through projects, case studies, role-plays, or labs	Some learners can demonstrate mastery over session/topic objectives by applying new skills through projects, case studies, role-plays, or labs AND Demonstrate their progress and understanding of important key points multiple times throughout the session	Most learners can demonstrate mastery over session/topic objectives by applying new skills through projects, case studies, role-plays, or labs AND Demonstrate their progress and understanding of important key points multiple times throughout the session via various modes	All learners meet descriptors for level 3

Figure 7.5: Career readiness competency: student-centered rubric sample. The organization is Generation: You Employed.

Career Readiness 1/2

	Emergent	Foundational	Advanced	Mastery
Social-Emotional Skills & Progress	Few learners can superficially articulate how social-emotional skills are important for success in their roles	Some learners can articulate in some depth how BSMs are important for success in their roles AND Conduct themselves with professionalism to mirror their future work environment	Most learners can articulate in depth how BSMs are important for success in their roles, conduct themselves with professionalism to mirror their future work environment AND Articulate their goals and connections with future career pathways	All learners meet descriptors for level 3 AND Monitor and articulate progress toward their goals
Relevance & Connections	Few learners can articulate how the content is relevant to their lived experiences and future role	Some learners can articulate how the content is relevant to their lived experiences and future role AND Are able to share their own experiences and knowledge with peers when prompted to further learning	Most learners can articulate how the content is relevant to their lived experiences and future role AND Are able to proactively share their own experiences and knowledge with peers to further learning AND Connect it with previously acquired content/skills via async and sync learning when probed	All learners meet descriptors for level 3 AND Independently connect it with previously acquired content/skills via both async and sync learning to further their own learning

Figure 7.5: Career readiness competency: student-centered rubric sample. The organization is Generation: You Employed.

- You'll never hear from every student during any one observation.
- Large cohort sizes can make it extra hard for instructors, coaches, or support staff to consider each learner individually.
- Some sessions will lend themselves to activities better suited for highlighting rubric items; some will not.
- Text descriptors for each line of the rubric can be subjectively interpreted, so comparing data between cohorts and programs is a challenge.

Those challenges are real, but they aren't deal breakers. They do not pose a big enough barrier that teachers should avoid trying to capture nontechnical skills in a qualitative way. As well, this rubric is just one tool Generation uses to drive a culture of learning and teaching. Excellent teachers know that the key to reaching the most students is presenting information and practice opportunities multiple times in various ways. The same holds true for how we evaluate our own practice and the actions of our learners that demonstrate its impact.

The language of core competency, of excellence in learning and teaching, of career readiness—that remains the same. The ways we apply, practice, and evaluate the impact of this common language varies often and is limited only by our creativity. With a common language in place, let's dig into additional classroom routines and strategies that drive success for educators and learners alike.

Reflections and Intentions

- Which of the eight NACE competencies resonate with you? Which feel challenging?
- What common language pieces are already alive in your classroom? Is this intentional or accidental? What aspects are missing?
- How can a shared understanding of career competencies and a culture of learning and teaching enhance your students' experiences in class? How can they enhance your feelings of success as their instructor?

8 Classroom Strategies to Increase Employability

"Education breeds confidence. Confidence breeds hope. Hope breeds peace."

—Confucius

Constraints on a teacher's time never cease. Secondary teachers may face pressure to only teach content taught on standardized tests. Vocational trainers may be expected to teach a certain way according to a certain curriculum. Mentors and career coaches may work on a push-in model where they have limited exposure to the students that need them the most.

Add these constraints, and the myriad others that accompany them, to the context in which we work: a changing world where jobs we know are fizzling out of the market, and new jobs yet to be conceived are taking their place. Artificial intelligence (AI) is evolving how we learn and create and prioritize—a truth that is both inspiring and alarming.

And, of course, class rosters are often overflowing, and prep time is never quite enough. We can have learners with needs we aren't equipped to meet sitting shoulder to shoulder with learners who are bored because they've already mastered what you began teaching yesterday.

In other words, teaching isn't for the faint of heart.

And that's okay.

To make significant improvements to your learners' future employability, you don't have to revolutionize your entire practice. You don't have to reinvent or restructure your course. You don't need to battle your administration for permission to step away from the approved course syllabus. Tiny changes, made consistently and with intention, can go a long way in bringing career preparation into a sustained and meaningful focus.

Increasing employability isn't a thing you do once. It's not something to check off your teaching to-do list. It's a vibrant, living aspect of classroom culture that honors the reality that one day, sooner or later, your learners will need to pursue, attain, and thrive in a career. This chapter will offer you a variety of strategies—some big and some small—for driving such a culture and increasing employability by doing so.

Three Strategies for Creating a Supportive Culture

Feedback and Reflection

Nurturing a culture in which feedback and reflection are present is key in any organization that wants to continuously improve. Entire books, seminars, and managerial training series are devoted to this. For our purposes, it is essential that it becomes automatic in the classroom and that a "test and learn" and "fail fast" mentality is in place.

If we want learners to process core competencies for career readiness, and if we want them to self-evaluate how well they are applying social-emotional learning (SEL), we need to give them tools fit for the task. By bringing real-world experiences into the classroom and by encouraging learners to get out of their comfort zones, we're pushing them gently toward the unknown. Vulnerability, fear, anxiety, discomfort—these are all understandable emotions that can surface when someone is facing their future in an ever-changing world. These feelings and emotions need to be acknowledged and honored in a way that, together with feedback on technical content, career competencies, and SEL, pushes learners forward toward hope and action.

Actions That Support a Culture of Reflection and Feedback

- Co-creating rubrics to identify the continuum of actions that will show varying degrees of proficiency when completing a certain project, task, or activity.
- Using those rubrics during and after the activity; providing time for self-grading, peer grading, and instructor feedback.
- Analyzing the points of difference in self-assessment and teacher assessment after a performance-based activity; communicating constructively and in an evidence-based way to come closer to a shared understand of performance.

- Using journals at the end of activities for learners to reflect on their own performance, considering what they would do differently next time, and making a commitment to how this will impact practice moving forward.
- Using online tools such as discussion forums or chats to reflect on experiences and deepening thinking.
- Encouraging peer-to-peer feedback; supporting such feedback sharing with protocols and conversation templates.

Put Yourself in the Shoes of a Recruiter and Employer

In Chapter 2, we discussed mindsets that support, motivate, and facilitate effective learning experiences that will serve students on their path to a career. The same mindsets matter here too—*and* it is important, while students are learning skills and practicing activities within the classroom, to think like a recruiter.

- If you were going to hire one of your students, what questions would you ask during a job interview?
- Can these questions be integrated into an existing activity, group project, or presentation?
- How can students reflect before, during, and after about why they are completing the activity?
- How can students articulate their thinking so that they can make explicit connections?

In a past role, I was responsible for recruiting teachers. To this day, I continue to interview educators regularly as well as support hiring processes for many other roles. Ask me to summarize best practices in interviewing, for teaching or most other professions, and I will highlight two elements that must be in place for the hiring process to be effective:

- Ask behavior-based interview questions. Past behavior is indicative of future behavior.
    - Tell me about a time when you made a mistake. How did you recover?

    - Describe a time that you worked with others to achieve a goal. What happened? What was your role in it, and what, if anything, would you do differently?
    - What is a new skill you have learned? How did you learn it, and how do you apply it in your daily life?
- Have applicants complete role-specific tasks (preferably on-demand) so that they can show what they know. Giving them feedback thereafter, and seeing how they respond, extends the value of the performance task.
    - For a sales role, perform a 2-minute pitch selling the product.
    - Participate in a hack-a-thon to show your coding skills.
    - Role-play with an interviewer to de-escalate an upset customer in a hospitality setting.

Variations of the preceding scenarios are endless and depend on the actual industry or job. Despite not being experts on all possible jobs, we can also assume they'll need to communicate their failures and accomplishments to show aptitude and growth. Therefore, if we facilitate these experiences within the classroom and explicitly name them as such, they'll have a touchpoint and some practice responding well in a critical moment.

Behavior-based interviewing rests on the assumption that the best indicator of future performance is past performance. On the surface, it may seem obvious and most anyone would agree it is fair; yet many interviewers still rely on more traditional question-and-answer formats alone. We can't know what kinds of interviews our learners will face. We do know that if they are faced with behavior-based interviews, we want them to know what's happening and why.

Effective behavior-based interviewing explores in detail a candidate's relevant past experiences to establish how they manage job responsibilities, engage with colleagues in times of success and failure, navigate obstacles, and rectify mistakes. Interviewers want to know:

- What beliefs, values, and patterns of thinking drive this candidate's outward behavior?
- How effectively is this candidate able to manage and learn from mistakes and failure?
- How well does this candidate manage change?

- In what ways has this candidate added to their team (or peers) in the past, and what is their capacity to add to this team?

Various organizations have created behavior-based interviewing frameworks that establish categories that are essentially social-emotional skills and mindsets. If candidates aren't tasked with demonstrating these skills and mindsets via a task, they will certainly be asked to talk about them and give examples of how they use the skills and embody the mindsets. At the end of the day, each hiring manager must know what kinds of questions to ask and why. As a teacher, you can also ask the right questions to support students in navigating the interviews that lie ahead of them in their career path.

Celebrate Failures

A classroom environment in which failure is celebrated and learned from is a place where real learning can happen. Failing fast and failing often are indicators that people are safe to innovate, explore, and push beyond their comfort zones. Who wouldn't want to learn in a place like that? However, it seems we do not always have learning environments that encourage this. Straight A's are lauded, and failures are (sometimes) triggers for remediation, to be accomplished alone or in small groups, quietly and away from the judging eyes of peers.

FROM THE PERSONAL ARCHIVE

I once attended a presentation from the founder of Spanx, Sara Blakely. Long before she was the founder of a billion-dollar-plus women's undergarment company, she was a door-to-door fax machine salesperson dreaming big while trying to make ends meet.

She shared that, as a child, each night at the dinner table, her dad would ask, "What did you fail at today?" He wasn't looking to berate his daughter for not excelling or bringing home a gold star. He was instead instilling a value that failing wasn't just okay; it was necessary to succeed, and it deserves to be discussed and praised. It's a part of life and absolutely essential if you want to grow.

These conversations shaped Sarah. I left the conversation inspired, not for my own growth, but for the growth of children. Since I thought her dad's nightly question was such a wonderful idea, I took it to our dinner table that very evening.

Without any introduction, I turned to our 8-year-old son and asked, "What did you fail at today?" I just dropped it right there. His response absolutely shocked me. It was like he had an allergic reaction to that question.

He threw up his arms and said, "Mom! Stop it! What are you talking about? I am not answering this question!"

I thought I'd been doing a great job promoting the importance of learning from our mistakes. I frequently asked him thoughtful reflection questions. I focused on praising effort and not outcomes. And that night, I was hoping to plant a seed—that this question would become a regular feature around the dinner table. Well, I was dead wrong.

My son hadn't received my message. Failure was not an option for him. He was *not* comfortable discussing it. Was this because he sees his own mom with perfectionist tendencies modeling the opposite behavior? Is this because his parents inadvertently put pressure on him to succeed? Whatever the reason, the result was the same. We had not put enough emphasis on how failure was essential to true success and not something to be avoided.

As we think about our own classrooms, we must consider what messages we are sending about failure. For example, how are learners treated when they answer a question wrong in front of peers? Who is celebrated most often in class, and under what conditions? Are we creating an environment of safety where progress beats perfection? Based on my experience with my son, if we think we're doing a good job celebrating failure, we should push ourselves to be sure that's the case. Decide first what evidence would show that the message is getting through, then objectively determine if that evidence is present in your class:

Actions That Celebrate Failure

- Highlight success stories of people in multiple industries who first failed—and failed big—before succeeding.
- While a learner provides a wrong answer to the question, frame your response as a win for the group. "I'm so glad you said that, Lisa. Your answer is understandable because <likely rationale

for the wrong answer>. You're not the only one who thinks this, I bet. This is helpful."

- Support class policies that honor progress. Allow learners to redo assignments and offer multiple chances to make a presentation.
- Design learning experiences that require students to be creative and ambitious. If a learner or a group misses the mark, have a frank discussion with them that doesn't involve guilt trips or shame. Objectively and calmly, get to the heart of the matter and give them a chance to improve.
- If your organization publicly praises top performers (honor roll, etc.), also formally praise learners whose progress is significant. The learner that went from a 50% average to a 70% average may have worked harder than the learner who went from an 85% to a 90% average.

So far, we've covered celebrating failures as it relates to a failed attempt at something done for class. In other words, how do you celebrate a failure that resulted from putting in effort that didn't pan out as expected? There is another aspect of failure worth considering—a powerful side effect that I've witnessed many times.

A culture of safety and courage, fostered by embracing failure and risk as a part of the learning process, can encourage learners to share more of their own personal challenges. This sets the stage for learners to understand themselves and their journey. Where once they saw failure, they may learn to see a story of triumph and growth. These moments can happen in whole-group, small-group, and one-to-one settings, and should always be student-led according to each individual's feelings of safety and interest in sharing.

These three strategies for creating supporting culture provide fertile ground for applying the strategies that follow. Let's now look at ideas and inspiration for practicing, discussing, and showcasing skills necessary for employability. Intentional, purposeful practice is a key component in the role-specific job training programs that I currently support, and whatever your setting, it is sure to impact your learner outcomes as well. Even though the next step in your student's journey might not be an immediate job, it is important to think about how students can "try on" different workplace situations, and practice technical and social-emotional skills in an integrated way.

Role Plays and Case Studies

Role-plays

Role-plays provide students with hands-on targeted practice and a way to demonstrate the integration of soft skills and technical skills. They are real-life situations where the student takes on the role of someone in a career. The goal is to practice solving the authentic workplace problem with a realistic solution.

Of course, it is easy for students to not take these experiences seriously. Acting in front of peers can feel unnatural, and laughing it off is an understandable and almost instinctive defense mechanism to that discomfort. Head this off by naming this upfront and then modelling role-plays yourself first; your vulnerability gives them a runway to engage more fully themselves.

When I first joined the workforce development industry, I will admit I was surprised that we were using these in the classroom with individuals 18-plus. However, I would listen to the students in class and at graduation who had felt that way, too—but then had a change of heart. One learner said, "I felt so silly acting out another character at first, but then I realized that my confidence increased because of the practice."

To maximize a role-play's benefits, embrace repetition. Have learners repeat the role-play—switching characters, going back to the character they've already played, even repeating the role-play back-to-back without changing the inputs.

And don't let online settings dissuade you, even if you are practicing for an in-person role. The goal of a role-play is to get as close to authentic practice as possible. And what is "possible" will change based on the context of your learning environment. In Figures 8.1 and 8.2, sample role-play session outlines offer a sequence of events for both settings.

In both settings, you will notice that repetition and feedback are essential components of the role-play. As well, provide clear guidance that technical and social-emotional skills are the integrated focus of the role-play. Figure 8.3 is a sample of role-play framing language and guidance for a Generation session that supports learners expecting to work in freelance roles. This role-play was designed for remote students taking the training virtually and synchronously with a cohort of peers.

In-person example:

- 5 min.—Frame the role-play, including rationale and expected outcomes.
    - Include refreshers about:
        - the purpose of role-plays.
        - guidelines for the practice.
        - guidelines for giving feedback.
- 1 min.—Move physically to be with your small group.
- 2 min.—Read through the handout and assign roles.
- 3 min.—Perform role-play according to scenario and character descriptions.
- 1 min.—Provide constructive feedback to peers.
- 4 min.—Switch roles, repeat the role-play, and provide constructive feedback.
- 4 min.—Switch roles, repeat the role-play, and provide constructive feedback.

Figure 8.1: Role-play protocol example: in-person format.

Online example:

- 5 min.—Frame the role-play, including rationale and expected outcomes.
- Include refreshers about:
    - the purpose of role-plays.
    - guidelines for the practice.
    - guidelines for giving feedback.
- 1 min.—Move to your breakout rooms.
- 2 min.—Read through the linked content and assign roles.
- 3 min.—Perform role-play according to scenario and character descriptions.
    - Consider having group members who aren't assigned a role turn off their cameras.
- 1 min.—Provide constructive feedback to peers.
- 4 min.—Switch roles, repeat the role-play, and provide constructive feedback.
- 4 min.—Switch roles, repeat the role-play, and provide constructive feedback.

Figure 8.2: Role-play protocol example: online format.

Students are next presented with a situation, based on a given role within a given profession, such as in Figure 8.4. They then respond to the prompts in real time. Afterward, they receive feedback on the variety of skills that they demonstrated.

- Professionalism, clarity, adaptability, and humility are four key principles for communicating clearly and effectively with clients.
- When receiving feedback from the client, it is important to respond professionally. This includes:
    - Listening actively.
    - Asking clarifying questions to understand the feedback better.
    - Showing appreciation.
    - Asking how you can improve.
    - Verifying you understand the specific steps to improve.
    - Demonstrating through your work that you heard the feedback and are trying their suggestions.
- Responding to feedback effectively means thinking through actions before taking them. Reacting to feedback impulsively is acting without thinking.
- High performers demonstrate:
    - The mindset of **personal responsibility** by thinking about what they say and how they say it.
    - The behavior of **client focus**, which means prioritizing client needs and preferences to deliver an excellent service or product.
- Those working in agencies will have colleagues to support communicating with clients. However, those who are freelancing will have to take complete ownership of the process.

Figure 8.3: Role-play framing content example. The organization is Generation: You Employed.

While students may need context on the given role to make meaning, this can be done for any profession. You can also get realistic situations from those you know in given fields or from business partners within the community. Teachers have the power to make these situations meaningful through the same practices that guide excellent teaching:

- circulating while students are working in small groups or popping into breakout rooms in virtual settings.
- giving positive reinforcement and constructive feedback.
- asking additional probing questions to push thinking.
- holding students to accuracy.
- offering evidence-based and realistic examples.
- ensuring active participation.

This will also increase student engagement given the relevance of the situations to real life. There's an element of excitement—and fun—when you situate students in real-life scenarios.

Situation

The Virtual Reality (VR) Developer is a freelancer who is building an interactive tour of a local botanical garden. The role-play begins as they finish presenting the expected experience to the client.

Role: Virtual Reality Developer

You are a recent university graduate and are building your reputation in the field of VR. After a referral from a friend, you have your first paying client.

You had completed a couple of basic prototypes of a virtual greenhouse for the client, and they were delighted. They decided they'd like to recreate the whole garden as an immersive VR experience. You accepted the job!

There are many zones in the garden, including indoor and outdoor spaces. It took a few weeks for you to build the environment of the greenhouse, and you now have only completed one of the five visualizations—and the deadline is approaching. You have lots of ideas for making this into an effective immersive experience and hope that your client will value the quality over quantity. You are confident you can build a great product and know you under-delivered this time around. However, you are also very nervous that you are about to lose your one and only client, and worry that they don't understand how difficult this product was to design.

Your goals in this role-play are to:

- Demonstrate effective communication skills when receiving feedback from a client.
- Respond to feedback.

Role: Client

You have taken a chance on a new VR Developer who is a friend of your daughter's from university. They are very affordable, but you are starting to worry that your projects are beyond their capabilities. The Developer just presented an incomplete product. Now, you will not be able to release the new tour on the timeline shared with your Board of Directors. You need to give them some tough feedback on the quality of their work and reiterate your expectations for the working relationship.

Your goals in this role-play are to:

- **Give the feedback** about the poor quality of the total product.
- If your freelancer **responds professionally to the feedback and takes personal responsibility**, share more suggestions and carry on with the contract.
- If your freelancer **does not respond professionally to the feedback and/or does not take personal responsibility**, say that this is not working out and you will need to cancel the contract.

Role: Observer(s)

Observe the interaction between the Developer and the client. Prepare to offer feedback on the following points.

Feedback prompts:

- What did the Developer do to respond to the client feedback?
- What did the Developer do to demonstrate personal responsibility?

Figure 8.4: Role-play scenario example. The organization is Generation: You Employed.

Case Studies

Cases studies are short, written stories that are based on authentic, challenging, on-the-job situations. Participants will read and discuss these stories in small groups to make conclusions about how to respond to these situations in their future role. The stories can be written to highlight exemplary or nonexemplary situations, and students analyze the characters' actions within the real-life scenario.

A teacher or trainer doesn't have to be an excellent writer to create a case study experience for their learners. A little research is all it takes via people in your extended network, or in reading blogs or articles that describe the role. Be mindful of your learners' reading levels as you prepare your case studies. This is not intended to be an assessment of how well a learner reads.

The more authentic a situation is presented on paper, the better. But don't let good be the enemy of great. Once you have implemented this strategy, you could even have students prepare their own case studies to share with their peers.

Case studies are typically facilitated in small-group discussions and then whole-group debriefs. This increases the vocal participation of more learners. In an online format, students can practice case studies using discussion boards asynchronously before meeting virtually to enjoy an active discussion. Or, you can encourage independent thinking and structure the experience to be self-led. Figure 8.5 is a sample agenda for a case study online protocol focused on an asynchronous, independently paced experience. Figure 8.6 is a sample case study based on a real workplace situation. Students are faced with analyzing and reacting to the situation and deciding what they would do differently.

The magic of a case study comes in the quality of the reflection questions. Excellent questions will push a learner to evaluate the specific actions and decisions of the main character, explicitly noting where technical and nontechnical skills were up to par—or not. Once you've drafted reflection questions, double check that your case study draft includes enough details that learners will have plenty to consider and discuss.

Time	Activity
4 min.	**Opening—independent work** ■ Participants review objectives ■ Participants reflect on key points
5 min.	**Reflection—independent work** ■ Participants answer reflection questions provided in relation to key points
5 min.	**Reading—independent work** ■ Participants read the case study
8 min.	**Case Study Questions—independent work** ■ Participants answer short-answer and multiple-choice questions about the case study
7 min.	**Discussion forum—asynchronous group work** ■ Participants share reflections on the course discussion board ■ Participants are tasked to return to the board at least twice to respond to their peers
1 min.	**Closing—independent work** ■ Participants

Figure 8.5: Generation example: case study protocol. The organization is Generation: You Employed.

Bring In the Learning and Take Out the Learning

Remember the young lady from the beginning of Chapter 7? The one who couldn't describe her own leadership experiences despite being a highflier, team trainer, and de facto manager at the fast-food restaurant? Imagine how her internship interview could have gone had she been guided to actively process her part-time experience with her teacher and peers beforehand.

By bringing in the learning, you'll shine a productive and forward-thinking light on your students' personal and work-based experiences. Be on the lookout for ways to bring student experiences from

Client 1: Thomas

Thomas is a 50-year-old wealthy businessman. He has noticed the growth of the AR/VR marketing campaigns in the last few years. He is currently exploring how these marketing campaigns can be used to build his business-a brand of home furniture. Due to his interest in the topic, he takes time to familiarize himself with different apps, experimenting with available platforms to understand how best he can use the same for his business. He decides to approach a freelancer to get his work started.

Client 2: Peter

Peter is a 22-year-old fashion designer. Fresh out of design school, Peter is eager to start his own label. A friend of his suggests that he can use filters to promote his brand. He explains that using filters can create a lot of hype and interest among the target audience. Peter is familiar with the filters he uses on some of his own personal social media accounts and thinks this is a great idea. He decides to approach a freelancer to get his work started.

Both the clients approach Joe, a freelance developer who understands the necessary AR/VR software and tools to work on their projects. Joe considers how to approach the project with the two new clients. Joe learns that Peter has very little knowledge on how technology has evolved and where it is headed. He prepares a presentation before the demo. Although Thomas has a technical background, Joe decides to share the evolution of technology with him as well. This saves Joe time since it's easier to prepare one presentation instead of two.

In two days' time, Joe conducts presentations and demos with both the clients explaining the impact of technology and its usage. He ensures that he uses only the allotted time expected for the demo. He also conducts dedicated meetings with the clients explaining the evolution of the technology and what lies in the future. At the end of a week, Peter hires Joe, but Thomas does not.

Reflection Questions:

What does Joe do well in managing client relationships?

What could Joe have done better with the client who did not hire him?

How can Joe resolve the issue now and still get the contract?

Why is it important for an AR Creator to understand client profiles and manage them well?

Figure 8.6: Generation example: case study. The organization is Generation: You Employed.

their outside lives into the classroom. The point is showing students that their experiences outside of school matter, can be integrated into the learning, and can help to grow their skills and shape their future career path.

Actions That Bring In the Learning

- Ask learners about their recurring commitments outside of school or your course. Consider all responses through the lens of employability: childcare, housework, part-time jobs, gig work. Model how to interpret those commitments as marketable skills.

  As learners get used to this kind of conversation, ask them to lead the discussion and frame each other's experiences through the lens of employability.

- Have learners share some of their earliest memories related to the world of work.

  What jobs did they admire as children?

  How does this connect to what they want for their future careers?

- Encourage learners to bring in job postings and company profiles for peer discussion. These can potentially be used to create case studies and role-plays, too!

Flipping it around, don't shy away from getting learners out into their communities to evaluate the world of work at their very fingertips. Depending on the context in which you teach, small or large local businesses may be interested in hosting learners for a tour of their workspace and a conversation about their industry. If that isn't available, see what students can learn about local businesses via the internet.

Heading out into the community can help students gain an understanding of different job environments and see all the different roles that workers can play. These trips can be combined with other school initiatives and activities, but it is important that the workplace lens is applied to these experiences. Ask questions such as: "How many different job roles did we observe? What were the primary responsibilities of those roles? What are the career pathways of those roles? What further research can we do to find out more about the roles?" The Activity Mapping questions you'll explore in Chapter 9, as well as empowering students to interview professionals, are powerful strategies to implement.

Actions That Take Out the Learning

- Ask around to see which local business are available to host learners for a tour of their workspace and a conversation about their industry.

- If that isn't available, see what students can learn about local businesses via the internet.
- If learners are able, task them with setting up visits or interviews with local professionals.
- For virtual courses, learners can find a job listing they would one day like to pursue. Have them research the company and prepare for an interview as if they were applying.
- Have learners select a role and do deep research regarding working conditions, salary ranges, and opportunities for advancement. Have them look within a 10- to 20-mile radius (or whatever makes sense given your geographical context) to see if any postings for that job or a related position are available. Encourage them to consider freelance and gig work when appropriate.
- Ask learners where they spend the most money or where they take their business—include both local brick-and-mortar businesses and online companies. In what roles and industries are these businesses? What is appealing and unappealing about related roles?
- Bring in guest speakers and prepare learners ahead of time by researching the individual and writing questions for their guest.

Of course, field trips are often hard to organize, and adult learners in training programs may not want to volunteer personal time for bonus excursions. Luckily, classroom technology can bring the workplace to us. Use video conferencing capabilities to virtually visit workplaces across the country or even the world to shadow workers and ask questions about their role, like what problems they are solving and what skills they apply daily.

Guest speakers can serve similar purposes to the workplace visits. Students can, and should, create interview guides for the guest speakers, researching their role and career path before their arrival. It's even possible that guest speakers could serve as mentors to students who take particular interest in the mentors' given careers.

Embrace AI in Your Teaching Practice

Innovation is everywhere when you unleash the power of AI within learning journeys and the craft of teaching. The speed of change is so great that by the time this book goes to print, there will be new and exciting applications of emerging technology that haven't even hit the market during my writing of the manuscript. Educators who open their minds to technology's innumerable possibilities will reap many rewards—from automated scoring of student work to digital teaching assistants to personalized learning journeys and generative AI-powered lesson plans. The future of teaching is bright and engaging.

There will be entire books, programs, and professional development opportunities devoted to training teachers how to leverage AI technology. As we are encouraging our students to deeply consider the impact of technology on the roles they pursue, we must ourselves do the same regarding the evolution of our own practice. Start somewhere now. Do not wait for a perfect opportunity to test what's out there, especially when free or low-cost options abound. Consider:

- Using generative AI to break down complex technical concepts in new and different ways than you or your existing program materials do.
- Allowing note-taking and summary applications to transcribe your online lessons so learners can easily revisit tricky content or class sessions missed due to absences.
- Watching the personalized learning space for innovations that could be easily adopted within your context; remediation or challenge activities and prompts can be generated quickly without you needing to start from scratch.
- Drafting session plans, presentation slides, assessment frameworks, and more first with AI so that your expertise and time can be spent polishing and preparing, rather than drafting.
- Researching industries and roles first with generative AI instead of search engines; let AI give you a first pass in answering interesting questions, and then validate the learning with complementary research.
- Seek out applications that can reduce the administrative side of teaching, such as taking attendance or gathering student profile data.

If there's an opportunity to focus more of your time and energy on the creative side of teaching, as well as the powerful and deeply human interactions between you and your students, investigate it with your eyes wide open. Make it a priority to learn from other forward-thinking educators, universities, and influencers who are energized by these innovations.

Micro-Moments for Increased Career Awareness

Role-plays, case studies, bringing in learning and taking out learning—these are high-impact ideas that do require a bit of preparation on the instructor's part. The following strategies can be pulled out of your toolkit at a moment's notice. They're great for impromptu discussions or moments when an activity ends early and you want to make the most of those extra few minutes.

Career Spotlights

Choose a weekly or monthly focus industry or role. Take 5–10 minutes to teach about the careers and pathways available within the career. Keep the role posted in the front of the room (or on an online discussion board) and come back to the role as time allows. Ask learners what appeals and what doesn't appeal about this career. Ask them to imagine a day in the life of a professional in this role.

Interview Question Bursts

Have behavior-based interview questions at the ready on stacked notecards or in an online document that learners have easy access to. Have peers ask one another the questions, and then record observations about their peer's responses. This activity can support on-the-spot thinking that is so frequently necessary in all aspects of life, not just employability.

Matching Problems to Careers

During students' conversations, listen to hear what problems they are facing, and what problems they'd like to solve. Consider the small and intimate ("My best friend owes me $50, and they won't give it up!")

to the large and complex ("I just hate thinking about climate change. We gotta do something about this.") Add to the conversation by talking about roles that are in any way related.

Be exhaustive, and don't shy from being humorous! In the first example, you could bring up lawyers, accountants, therapists, greeting card designers (who may write the perfect sentiment about maintaining friendships by honoring promises), coffee shop owners (who can serve you coffee while you have an honest talk with your friend).

In the second example, the list is endless: Politicians, scientists, packaging designers, farmers, lobbyists, home builders. . . . You're only limited by your imagination.

The goal is to pique interest and open up just how vast the career world is. Have predictable questions at the ready to extend the thinking about the career: what are the working conditions? How much does it pay? What are the career opportunities beyond the entry-level job? Are there internship opportunities? How many people across the world are in those jobs today?

Increasing a focus on employability in your classroom or training program doesn't require a complete redesign of your syllabus or scope and sequence. Small actions, done with intention, will have a big impact. Instead of relegating career conversations to other departments or career centers or anyone else you hope will pick up the baton, commit to doing what you can to get your students ready for the workplace.

Your students could be years or days away from actively pursuing work, but the seeds you plant today will continue to grow. As the adage goes, if you want a fully grown tree, the best time to sow the seed was 10 or so years ago. The next best time? Right now.

SPOTLIGHT STORY

One student works on composing a social media post to generate more traffic to a local company's website. Another makes a phone call to that same company to set up a client meeting. Two other students discuss how to approach pitching their idea for an app to help the company onboard new employees. For students enrolled in the Wauwatosa and Elmbrook School Districts' innovative LAUNCH program, working in teams to fulfill a project for a real local company is not an anomaly. It is the norm.

When it comes to engaging students in their learning with authentic practice, the Wisconsin school districts exemplify how we can empower students with the skills they need to find success in their future careers. The idea for LAUNCH originated with Mark Hansen, superintendent of the Elmbrook School District. Hansen pitched the idea in response to problems he saw in his high-achieving school district. He observed a loss of engagement by seniors who felt their high school experience had nothing else to offer them. He also saw students not coming back to the community after college. With the pipeline of young, local talent drying up, the business district struggled to thrive. Hansen's goal was to fight apathy by finding a way to make the last year of high school meaningful by engaging students in their community and, thus, enticing young people to make Brookfield home. The answer was LAUNCH.

The district's LAUNCH program offers students the opportunity to explore professions, learn professional skills, and get real-world experience while also fulfilling their state's graduation requirements. Juniors and seniors can choose from 15 "strands" that blend traditional core content with electives that feature real-world professional experience. For instance, students who enroll in the Law and Public Policy strand will take AP Language and Composition, but they will also take Mentorship, Current Issues as well as Crime, Society, and Law. Through the experience, students can expect to embrace profession-based learning, responsiveness, self-discovery and exploration, professional skills development, and an entrepreneurial mindset.

I spoke with Patrick Perez, a veteran teacher of 28 years and a LAUNCH instructor for the past 7, about his experiences with the program and how it has transformed his teaching as well as his students' lives. Perez entered the program at the ground level and has seen it transform into the robust and effective program it is today.

When asked about his initial decision to help get LAUNCH off the ground, Perez expressed how leaving his traditional role behind to embark on a new professional path required a "big leap of faith." The transition came with challenges and uncertainty. He had concerns about how to meet the standards of the English curriculum while also aligning with the goals of the program. Perez noted that making such a move without the certainty of success "is scary for teachers." Perez began with facilitating the English + Global Business Strand

and now also runs Law and Public Policy as well. His teaching practices provide a model for how to facilitate a program that collaborates closely with the community.

The heart of LAUNCH resides in its real-world, project-based learning that blends application of core content with the skills needed to thrive in a rapidly changing workplace. Students learn professional skills and then apply them with actual clients in the community.

In a traditional language and composition course, students often find it difficult to see the connection between their writing, research, speaking, and listening assignments and how they can apply those skills in their future careers. But in Perez's Global Business program, students engage with the course material in a way that feels more meaningful to them.

Instead of traditional classroom presentations, students learn effective professional speaking skills by working together to meet the needs of a client. Students write pitches for clients that provide them with authentic practice in writing to communicate and persuade. They plan, create, and deliver presentations to local companies, participate in meetings with clients, and "pick up the phone" to get help with a project. Rather than showing their research skills in a paper, students conduct research to answer questions and help solve problems. They ask reflective and metacognitive questions about the research: "I need an answer. How do I find my answer? How do I know it is a valid answer?"

As Perez emphasizes, collaborating with actual clients gives students an idea of what work "looks like for people in the real world." The projects students work on through LAUNCH have an "entrepreneurial aspect," says Perez; students have to "show storytelling and creativity."

In the Global Business strand, Perez notes while the specifics of the projects students work on vary, they often follow "predictable patterns." For instance, a company needs an event planned. They want a presence at a certain conference, and it is the students' job to determine the logistics of how to set it up, what to put out for the conference, and who oversees putting it together. Students make promotional materials and create social media posts. They learn how to professionalize posts for a specific audience and get to see the immediate impact of their work.

Other clients may include a company with an international presence that wants to send people to other countries to do work and needs a streamlined process for helping newer employees going on their first trip overseas to acculturate to their unfamiliar environment. Students may work with a local insurance agency who needs and requests a specific number of meetings with potential clients. Students write a script together and learn to cold call.

Perez exclaims that the "coolest projects are ill defined." Such projects require students to use creativity, problem solving, and teamwork. In one project, someone suggested the company could give their employees a paper brochure to help navigate their travels overseas, and the students pointed out that the employee would not be carrying a crumpled-up piece of paper and instead suggested a mockup for an app. Students consistently use professional skills that help make them more employable while also exploring potential careers.

Perez notes that the Law and Public Policy strand is "an outlier since clients do not come in with projects." Due to the nature of the profession, students cannot study ongoing legal cases. However, students still get to work with clients and receive real-world experience thanks to a local law firm that has partnered with LAUNCH and has been particularly generous with its time.

The firm brings in people to show students how a contract works and how to put one together. They disseminate information on litigation and provide briefs on past cases. Students then get to write up claims. Students have even had the opportunity to observe a criminal trial with a trial lawyer "at their side giving them the 'inside baseball.'"

Companies and sponsors seem eager to participate in the program and support students. Perez says that to get companies and sponsors interested in partnering with the district, the students write pitches. "We ask them to think of the tenth thing that you never get to and let our kids take a crack at it." The strategy clearly works. LAUNCH partners invest in students, and students participate in the process from conception to finished project.

One of the essential skills students learn through participating in LAUNCH is teamwork. When I asked how he teaches teamwork, Perez says that "the businesses brought what was needed." In fact, a local company—Direct Supply Team—took part in teaching students the core values of teamwork. The company has an intensive training program that it takes their employees through. The company shares with students how to work in teams, including the setting of norms and fulfilling a role on a team.

As Perez notes, in a typical classroom, teachers put students together, give them a task, and do their best to make sure all students are participating and "one dominant person isn't taking over." Students "know they are jumping through hoops to meet the outcome for you." In contrast, Perez says that by participating in the business world, students learn that "there are real consequences if teams do not work together."

Perez emphasizes that students learn to navigate the interpersonal challenges that occur when people work together in a "high-stakes" atmosphere. They discover that to start to work well in a group, they need to have norms. Students no longer see the process as "jumping through hoops." Rather, they see it as an opportunity to talk and to reflect.

When issues arise, students discuss how feelings of disempowerment and anger can come up when working with others, and hash out what they can do proactively in a group to ensure it does not happen again. Perez states, "I never did that in a classroom." In a traditional classroom, the focus stays on content and trying to get through the curriculum or finishing the project because another "unit is looming." He notes that group work does not get "its due time" in these environments, but "in the LAUNCH program, the program will not work if we do not." Students' engagement in learning teamwork through authentic practice exemplifies what it means to shift teaching forward.

I was also curious about what the experience is like for teachers in LAUNCH, and what qualities teachers need to be successful in the program. Perez states that teachers need to be able to "go with the flow and function in an environment" that they cannot dictate. Educators need to be "willing to give up a lot of control that teachers tend to prize." In LAUNCH, teachers have more of a facilitator role. As Perez notes, educators often "talk a lot about being facilitators of learning," but to thrive in a program like LAUNCH, educators "have to be" effective facilitators.

Instead of designing assessments, learning experiences, and procedures, teachers must shift their process and their conception of their role in the classroom. Perez says he is honest with kids about how they cannot come to him with every question because he does not know every answer. Instead, he tells them that he can help them figure out whom to ask, where to look for answers, and what those answers might look like.

As a result of the shift in teaching practices, Perez underscores how the "classroom atmosphere and relationship you have with students is entirely different than the normal classrooms." He reports how students have said, "I felt like you were working alongside me. We were working toward the same goal. When we went into the meeting and it went well, you were as excited as us."

Perez's description of his classroom interactions highlights the joy students have in learning because of the camaraderie, autonomy, and authentic practice created in the program—an atmosphere that is difficult to foster in a typical classroom. Perhaps this environment is why the program has no shortage of willing educators. Perez points out that even though transitioning from the traditional classroom to LAUNCH is a professional risk, no teachers in the program have wanted to go back to the regular classroom setting. He does advise that it is best for first- and second-year teachers to get experience in the regular classroom before embarking in a program like LAUNCH.

Perez says his experience in the LAUNCH program has even influenced his own non-LAUNCH classrooms. He now provides students with more autonomy, voice, and choice—classroom practices that mimic more of a workplace atmosphere and bridge students' transition to careers.

Most importantly, the LAUNCH program provides opportunities for students that empower them and have even changed their life trajectory. Perez relates the story of a student who was chronically absent from school and was really struggling in his regular classrooms. He discovered that he loved business. He would skip his morning classes but show up early to attend LAUNCH in the afternoon. He would show up "sharply dressed in a suit jacket, he was so into it." He loved getting out of the classroom and working with actual professionals, and Perez would see him "stand up straighter."

Perez discusses how when kids have the opportunity to explore different professions, they can make more informed decisions about their future. In some cases, Perez argues, "Giving them this opportunity to try things out really saved them time and money."

He relates how one young woman thought she wanted to go into the field of psychology or social science. After completing a project with Milwaukee Tool that involved engineering, specifically circuit boards, she decided she wanted to study engineering in college instead. Another student discovered they did not want to major in business after their experiences. Students leave the program with a better understanding of themselves, including where their strengths and passions reside.

The program's mission statement summarizes the program best: LAUNCH "represents the collaboration of education, business and community, providing students with a unique, immersive experience, resulting in high skilled, adaptable, global innovators and leaders." And as Perez's experiences in the program exemplify, the program engages and supports students in not only thinking about their future careers, but also in offering them a space to gain authentic practice with professional skills relevant to their future goals—whether they plan to attend college or immediately enter the workforce.

LAUNCH and the teachers who facilitate the learning enable the program to thrive. They have much to teach us about moving our own teaching practices forward and taking that first "leap of faith" in implementing authentic practice that supports students in their transition to work.

Reflections and Intentions

- What opportunities have your students had lately to reflect on the world of work? What would you like to implement into an upcoming project?
- How does failure look and feel in your classroom or training setting?
- Select an upcoming task or activity; think about how you can augment it by wearing the hat of a recruiter. What real-world questions might you ask?

9 Developing Curriculum Where Employment Comes First

"Do not let what you cannot do interfere with what you can do."

—John Wooden

Great curriculum comes from a variety of sources. Many excellent teachers are also outstanding curriculum designers and love to design assets that precisely bring their vision to life. Other teachers benefit from curriculum developed elsewhere, designed for them to implement while personalizing it with their own special touch. When curriculum is required to increase employability, its design must account for the multifaceted needs of the role or industry in question as well as the local culture and jobs market into which learners will graduate. This is true regardless of who is designing the curriculum.

This chapter will provide an overview of one such curriculum development process, highlighting the elements that support improved employability. Regardless of your role in the curriculum development process, understanding this approach can help you to supplement, augment, or even improve the design of the curriculum used within your context. This chapter will cover the following components of a curriculum development process for high-impact employability programs.

Essential Curriculum Design Components for Enhancing Employability

- Know your audience.
- Deeply understand the targeted role to the level of daily activities and skills.

- Gather additional data about the role.
- Identify the breakdown moments for the targeted role; connect those moments to the program's performance goals.
- Create an assessment plan.
- Select employability skills that will be taught in addition to the role's "hard" skills.
- Design an interactive learning journey.

The Employability-Focused Curriculum Design Process

Know Your Audience

When preparing a speech, presentation, or written documentation, one golden rule of communication reigns supreme: ABC—Audience Before Content. The importance of knowing the audience may seem obvious, but it is often missed. The key to leading exceptional learning experiences is knowing whom you are reaching, what they need to hear, and how they need to hear and experience it. Curriculum design has at least two audiences it must consider—the instructor and the learner. There is much to be said about designing curricula that are supportive of instructors, but this chapter will focus more on the learner as the primary audience.

The attention (or lack thereof) spent on understanding your learner shows up in all parts of their experience in the classroom. Thinking about how they will receive and interact with the implemented curriculum design is essential. If curriculum doesn't meet their needs, what is the point? A prior teaching mentor of mine used to say, "If nobody learned anything, then nobody really taught anything." I'd feel uncomfortable when she'd say that, but my discomfort stemmed from acknowledging the truth in the sentiment.

In curriculum design, fostering connection between learners and classroom experiences helps learners feel like they can see themselves in the curriculum. This may mean that they can relate to any characters or scenarios in the curriculum and that the tone and language used is appropriate and accessible. They need to feel the curriculum is relevant to their life—both the "hard" skills that are needed to conduct the basic functions of a job, but as well, the soft skills learned through social-emotional learning (SEL) that will make them strong and successful candidates for promotion. Understanding their existing prior knowledge, and their actual level of incoming interest, is also critical to keep them from being either bored or overwhelmed.

Understanding your primary audience—the learner—is more easily accomplished when the design team creates learner personas. Developing detailed, prototypical profiles that embody the expected learner is a common practice in product development across industries. Outside of education, each persona is a profile or description of who the user or customer is, what they are bringing to the experience, and what their needs may be.

The following questions can help build a draft of the expected learner persona:

- What is their basic demographic information (age, familial status, dependents, living situation, etc)?
- How do they spend their time now, and what does a typical day look like?
- What access do they have to technology, and what are their tech skills?
- What are their short-term and long-term goals?
- What are their needs and challenges (include concrete needs as well as social-emotional needs; both a sense of belonging and access to Wi-Fi, for example, merit attention)?
- What are their attitudes and beliefs coming into the program?
- What is their level of education and work experience?

Your program's stakeholders and comprehensive context will determine how the answers to the preceding questions will impact the curriculum. Considerations can include timing of program delivery, how the curriculum is delivered (in person, online, or hybrid/blended format), the daily schedule, the duration of the program, the literacy level of the curriculum, and more.

Take a moment to jot which questions would be relevant to answer for your own context. If you have a heavy hand in curriculum development, consider how a persona draft will enhance your design work. If you do not directly impact curriculum design, consider how understanding this profile will better support your teaching preparations in advance of your next cohort.

Conducting focus groups is another effective strategy. This involves asking supervisors to bring small groups of employees together to discuss their experiences. This could be a group of high performers or low performers, based on the goal or questions you seek to answer. (Of course, *never* share with the focus group members if the group has been deemed low- or high-performing.)

Once, I was sitting in a conference room at a call center with a group of employees a supervisor deemed as "high performers." These individuals exceeded the expectations of the job, were on track to be promoted, and were often asked to train new joiners. These were the employees that supervisors would hire again in an instant.

I sought to understand the ins and outs of the role and their specific strategies for overcoming make or break moments on the job; selfishly, I wanted to make sure these strategies became part of the curriculum. When I asked what the hardest parts of the job were, one employee said it was the monotony of it. "You just have to keep answering call after call, hour after hour."

I asked, "What do you do so that it is not so boring?" One person shared that they have a whiteboard at their desk, and they make a tally mark after each call as it motivates them to see all they have accomplished. Suddenly, 5 or so of the 10 people shouted, "I do that too!" Everyone had the same shocked look on their faces. They didn't know they were all using some of the same strategies to cope with monotony. They continued with other great strategies that tapped into a positive outlook on life, self-awareness, and stress management (e.g., self-talk, doing puzzles). Gathering these strategies and including them in the subsequent curriculum empowered many other students who would go on to face these exact challenges.

Deeply Understand the Targeted Role to the Level of Daily Activities and Skills

Skills Mapping is a common human resources (HR) exercise that takes the job responsibilities from a job description and creates a representation of the skills needed for the given role. HR teams often map that representation against the current skills within their workforce. At my current organization, Generation: You, Employed, we do something similar that takes Skills Mapping one step further.

Generation is a global nonprofit organization that supports career seekers in multiple countries. Our vision is of a future wherein a meaningful career and sustained well-being is available for every person, anywhere in the world. Our established practice of "Activity Mapping" uses job shadowing and multiple interviews to determine the specific activities of a current role. It goes beyond the job description to paint a picture of the daily activities for a professional in the role. I have had the opportunity to travel the world shadowing individuals in their jobs and get a solid sense of their day-to-day activities, the demands of their work, and the strategies they use to overcome the difficult aspects of the role. I have shadowed roles within hospitals, hotels, factories, offices, and more. These experiences have positively impacted the way I think about job readiness, career success, and curriculum design and delivery.

During the Activity Mapping process, we spend several hours shadowing many people in and near the given role across multiple employers to get a realistic industry view of the work. When the job shadowing occurs, it is good for the conditions to be as realistic as possible. This includes observing during the busiest times while, of course, being as nonobtrusive as possible to allow for the flow of business. The following is a short description of the activities within Generation's Activity Mapping process:

- **Interview** direct managers and other experts to understand the job activities of the role.
- **Observe** ~10–20 people, for ~4–6 hours each, to understand the job activities/interactions required by the role.
- **Conduct several focus groups** with top, middle, and bottom performers to gather details about how top performers approach job activities differently from middle and bottom performers.
- **Create a list of job activities and breakdown moments** using these inputs to highlight "what good looks like" and "common gaps" in the technical skills, behavioral skills, and mindsets that differentiate top performers in the role.
- **Refine the list of job activities and breakdown moments** by sharing it with employer partners and gathering feedback.

Getting down to the daily activity level provides the rich details needed to determine what performance goals will be pursued across a program. A bullet point on a posted job description might say "administrative duties." This could mean a variety of things. By observing the actual administrative tasks in real time, we can understand the level of difficulty, pre-requisite skills, and other related aptitudes necessary for success. For example, composing an email requires a level of English proficiency, adaptive communication skills, professionalism in communication, and the ability to compose, send and attach documents within an email application. Some professionals fly through emails with ease while others struggle. This includes both technical skills and "softer" skills such as communication and professionalism. That's a much richer view than simply seeing "written communication skills" on a job description. Pairing this depth of understanding with the learner personas previously described offers designers a chance to hack the content and make it targeted, efficient, and highly relevant.

Throughout this chapter, I'll use an example from the hospitality industry to break down certain components of the curriculum development process. This is a role that Generation has supported in the past—that of a front desk agent role within the hospitality industry. This role greets and supports guests during the check-in process and attends to their other needs during a stay at the hotel. Like nearly every other industry, technology is disrupting this work. That's another invaluable benefit of robust Activity Mapping—by staying connected to employers and returning to the results of your mapping, you can stay current with recent innovations and applications of new technology.

Here are some of the key activities of this role as determined by Activity Mapping. Consider how this level of detail can help you understand the skills necessary for success on the job. Note: the complete list of activities is always very long. This is unavoidable if the goal is to comprehensively capture the fullness of each job role. Figure 9.1 is an abridged sampling of the front desk agent role, abridged here to offer a sense of the level of detail that is included.

Again, these are only a few job activities. After synthesizing our Activity Mapping findings into a comprehensive activities list, we further refine the specific steps needed to execute that job activity to the smallest level of detail. This may mean capturing the standard operating procedure and/or the processes used by high performers and approved by supervisors. The detail helps us to really understand how the activity authentically gets completed thanks to the specific skills an individual needs to perform to execute on that activity.

Key Job Activities: Front Desk Agent, Hospitality

Guest Check-in: Hospitality associates are the first point of contact that a guest has with the hotel. They are responsible for welcoming the guest, performing data entry to check the guest into the hotel, answering questions about hotel amenities and policies, and potentially cross-selling or upselling products or services.

Answer Phone and Direct Calls: Answering the phone professionally and efficiently is a key and consistent task for a hospitality associate. This may be the first time a guest contacts the hotel for a reservation, or it may be an existing guest who just needs some information.

Cash Handling: Associates are often responsible for a point of sale (POS) station and/or for operating a cash register efficiently, which may include handling cash in addition to credit and debit cards, and other forms of payment.

Handling Guest Complaints: Sometimes, guests are unhappy with their accommodations, the amenities of the hotel, or some other aspect of their experience. It is the responsibility of a hospitality associate to de-escalate these situations and resolve guest complaints in a way that is professional and within reason for the hotel. Front desk agents must also know where their responsibility and authority end, and when to engage their managers in solving customer needs.

Execute Cross-sell/Upsell Opportunities: When it becomes evident that a guest could benefit from either a better, or additional product, front desk agents must be able to cross-sell/upsell a customer while providing real value; this is a great skill for a front desk agent to possess to help make the guest happy while increasing the amount of money they spend at the hotel's location.

Figure 9.1: Key job activities for front desk agent, abridged. The organization is Generation: You Employed.

The core of Activity Mapping is to get people to articulate their knowledge and actions so that the learning of such can be replicated by others. However, the process can get complicated because we are pursuing understanding that goes beyond explicit knowledge. Explicit knowledge here means concrete and absolute facts that can be defined and easily expressed in spoken word or on paper. If the actions performed on a job could be easily articulated and then replicated through simple memorization and regurgitation, job training programs would need only to practice memorization and regurgitation. Instead, we aim to identify the implicit or tacit knowledge—the kind of skills and understanding that most often come from personal experience or deep, authentic practice.

In our hospitality example, there is incredible tacit knowledge required to de-escalate a situation with an upset customer. We can teach the steps to follow when customers get angry; however, it is difficult to capture the wisdom and intuition that a high performer uses to turn around the situation. How do they use eye contact and read body language? How do they know when to insert a comment, and when to remain silent? It's the difference between a detail-oriented, novice cook who can dutifully follow a recipe to decent results compared with a veteran, expert chef who cooks incredible dishes by smelling, tasting, and feeling. No classroom or training program can promise a veteran, master chef on day one (literally, or figuratively). But every attempt to go beyond explicit knowledge gets the new professional one step closer.

This is why observation is so important when seeking to understand job activities and challenges before shaping them into training experiences. We watch how people perform tasks and ask the right questions to get them to verbalize the difficult-to-explain processes in order to help more people achieve at the same situational outcomes.

At the stage of gathering evidence on job activities, we resist analyzing all the data just yet. It is important to wait to gather further inputs from multiple employees in the role, cross-check those findings with the other interviews, and then vet those findings with industry employers who *didn't* participate in Activity Mapping. However, you can start to identify the technical skills (e.g., cash handling) and the softer skills (e.g., handling guest complaints) even as the full process is completed. Technical and soft skills are given equal weight since you cannot be successful in the role without each skill set. Moreover, it is essential to integrate the technical skills with the soft skills. When we teach the steps to de-escalating an upset customer, we also teach the skills of customer focus and stress management. When we give learners the opportunity to practice these skill types together, there is a greater chance that it will translate to performance on the job.

Gather Additional Data about the Role

Even when it is not possible to engage in a full Skills Mapping or Activity Mapping, you and your learners can explore targeted roles in innovative ways. Push your learners to go past their preconceived notions of what a role is and how it is performed. In doing so, they can get closer to understanding the role's authentic daily realties as opposed to a best-case, idealized version they may hold in their minds.

Go Online

If you or your students are not able to talk directly with professionals in the role or those in the hiring journey that leads to that role, get as close as you can by digging into job postings online. Use websites like LinkedIn, Indeed, Monster, Zip Recruiter, and Glassdoor to search for roles, and do a close reading of the job descriptions to pull out key themes and requirements. Doing this yourself as you prepare for a unit will bring its own value; teaching your students to do so on their own further amplifies the benefits.

Make sure learners track job requirements, including certifications, trainings, degrees, and work experience. Look for similarities in requirements for related roles between different types of companies. Do additional research into these elements on their own to see what's involved. From costs to timing to hidden requirements, shine a light on the path that leads to a successful job hunt. Consider grouping learners who are keen to explore different roles within an industry to see similarities and differences.

When roles describe previous work experience, encourage yourself and learners to do similar explorations for the type of roles that would *provide* such prior experience. Every layer of understanding is a building block in their path to a role. Encourage learners to look for skills requirements, including SEL skills that may be described in language different than your learners are used to.

If you or your learners find it hard to find openings or job descriptions for certain roles, lean into that observation. Ask yourself why these posts aren't plentiful. Are these roles hard to find? Are they posted under different titles or search terms than what's in use? Are there geographic dead zones or hot spots for this profession? Each question offers important considerations for learners to bear in mind. If they can't find accessible job openings now, what will change—or not change—when they are through with training or school and are searching in earnest? The answers may be hard to face, but better sooner rather than later when the stakes are higher.

Don't be afraid to let generative AI give you and your learners a head start on some of this research, as well. Work with your students to create excellent, detailed prompts to feed into AI-powered search applications. You may ask, "In a typical workday, how often does a small business owner who runs a retail store face challenges with customers, and what skills are useful for solving the most common customer incidents?" The response may not be completely reliable, but it could give your learners a jumpstart on something to further verify, or a new angle to pursue related to understanding a role and the skills it requires. You can use traditional research or interviews to validate the learnings generated by AI.

Go Live

Once your learners have gathered a list of skills and other requirements for the roles, think about ways they can live out these skills in simulations and role-plays. Create scenarios—or have students create scenarios for one another—that provide a chance to act out these skills within the context of the job role. Consider the setting in which the work will be performed and what other teammates will be involved in accomplishing key tasks.

As discussed in Chapter 8, making the most out of role-play experiences requires guiding your students through discussions and repeat performances. Here, create a simple role-play by taking one discrete skill noted in a job description and imagining a work-based scenario where the professional in the role uses that skill. Then, after acting out that moment, ask students how they felt pretending to use the skill. If a skill or attribute such as communication or teamwork were the role-play's focus, ask them to break down that skill into observable actions or words. This may feel difficult at first; encourage them to get specific, even if it feels over the top or silly. Once they've more specifically named observable actions or words, have groups repeat their role-plays, giving more focus to the small skills that add up to the essential trait or ability named in a job description.

Encourage your students to internalize job description requirements through role-plays, presentations, peer discussion, and deep reflection. By structuring classroom activities and projects that do the same, you're showing them how valuable it is to understand the core requirements of a role—both technical and social-emotional.

Another strategy that can help students imagine the daily life in and skills required of a role: have them look to their existing work life and analyze their current skills, including noting the evidence they can point to that demonstrates these skills. Early in my teaching career, my principal sent me to a leadership training to support my supplemental duties working with my peers through teacher coaching. One element of the training was being taught how to analyze my tasks to shine a light on how my time was spent. Prior to the training, I thought, "I mentor and coach new teachers. I observe, I talk to them, and I document the whole thing." The training helped me realize that each of those elements involved lots of smaller skills, each of which took time and called on an area of expertise.

Guide learners to do the same for any part-time work they already do, including work at their homes such as babysitting, meal preparation, and other housework. This is aligned with the guidance previously shared about guiding learners to reflect on their current skills and assets to market themselves for great opportunities. This practice not only helps them understand their own existing skills and their value to employers; it also helps them to think critically and discretely about how time is spent. Building this muscle will heighten their ability to research opportunities, estimate time, and infer aspects about the role they are pursuing.

Go Social

Encourage the use of Twitter/X or other social media platforms to search for blog posts, industry news, big names, and other content about the role and its industry. If the role in question has influencers or popular voices who share content about their work, encourage a deep dive into their archives. Also, encourage learners to reach out to people who are accessible online with targeted questions. (Of course, a primer on professional written communication is a great precursor here.) If, at first, social networks aren't offering much content of interest, have learners return to the skills and work experience needed as previously discovered; use those terms to unearth interesting inputs.

Beyond popular social networks, there are professional networks and organizations that support the industry or targeted role. Local, regional, and national organizations will have different content and options available for public consumption, and some may be open to connecting your class or grads to content or individuals who can prove influential. If you are teaching in an area where the role in question does not have consistently strong hiring demand, encourage your students to look to other geographical areas—as they also consider how this reality could impact their future and career decisions.

Identify the Breakdown Moments for the Targeted Role; Connect Those Moments to the Program's Performance Goals

When it comes to breakdown moments, at Generation, we figure out the most challenging aspects of a role—the moments that often cause employees to quit or get fired. Then, we create program performance goals designed to overcome those points of potential failure—the breakdown moments. Exposing learners to the most challenging aspects of a role helps learners have grounded expectations and also pursue important growth areas.

Identifying breakdown moments is accomplished through the rich investigations, shadowing, and interviews that compose our Activity Mapping processes. Short of that level of insight, it will be hard for you or your learners to identify these moments. That's okay. They may need to make educated guesses about what makes or breaks professionals in this work. And the richer the research thus far, the more informed those educated guesses are.

Continuing with the hospitality example, Figure 9.2 shows one breakdown moment that was identified across multiple employers; note that for the full program, multiple breakdown moments were identified and addressed through program content.

If actual breakdown moments are hard to pinpoint due to lack of access to professionals in the role, guide learners to brainstorm possible breakdown moments using their own experiences and learnings. For example, if they engaged in role-plays to internalize required skills as

Breakdown Moment	What Makes This Challenging for the Role
Maintaining professionalism in tense and/or exhausting situations	■ Long working shifts ■ Working on holidays ■ Standing for long periods of time ■ Meeting dress code expectations ■ Needing to always be professional regardless of the situation and even when in a rush

Figure 9.2: Sample breakdown moment: front desk agent. The organization is Generation: You Employed.

noted on a job description, offer the following questions to bring out even more insight from the activity:

- What was the most challenging moment of that role-play?
- How did you feel during those moments?
- What stress could this role bring to your life?
- What factors could impact whether a day at work here would be stressful? Is there a busy season, or periodic deadlines, for example?

Many roles and industries have similar moments that lead to failure or stress. Encourage students to consider the following potential situations and estimate whether this would impact their ability to stay in the role. Imagine . . .

- feeling pressure from your peers or managers to keep up with timelines.
- not completing the task in the required time (in roles that feature task-based work).
- having to be at work—on time—very early every day with no exceptions.
- dressing professionally consistently.
- having restrictions on your calendar due to limited vacation time.
- receiving critical feedback from managers and peers when you are first learning the ropes.

Push learners to think about why these challenges could impact them. What is the root cause of their potential discomfort? Is the root cause something that can be overcome with improved technical or SEL skills? Or is this an indicator that they need to more closely explore the role to make sure it is really a potential fit? For example, imagine the targeted role requires strict timeliness, and your learner knows they are always late. Would intentional planning around personal morning routines or planning your transportation route to work make a difference? Because this is a practice they can do and test now while still in school or training, they'll gain insight into themselves long before critical job decisions need to be made.

If you are investigating breakdown moments to inform a role-specific training program, be sure to embed these learnings into your program-wide architecture. Connect this to the goals of your program by naming the skills needed to overcome the challenge; then, integrate those skills into your units and sessions. For example, if a common theme across the roles researched is "communication skills," and related breakdown moments involve using professional, respectful language, as well as nonverbal communication skills, name those as goals and offer guided instruction and numerous practice opportunities across the student experience.

Create an Assessment Plan

At Generation, we use the backwards design approach as outlined in *Understanding by Design* by Grant Wiggins and Jay McTighe. Understanding by Design (UbD) means starting with performance goals first instead of starting with the learning activities and then building toward summative outcomes. For nearly 20 years, educators have leveraged this design methodology to ensure that content taught scaffolds toward a predefined end goal. This is a key strength of the most exceptional educators I have worked with; they always start with the end in mind and structure learning experiences that will lead to students being able to perform the desired end goals.

After the performance goals are articulated, the assessment strategy needs to be conceived, followed by the design of the learning activities. Consideration should be paid to both formative and summative assessment. The following questions can jumpstart the process of determining the assessment strategy:

- How will we know whether a student can demonstrate these skills successfully at the end of the program? (summative)
- How will we know if they can demonstrate them successfully all along the course of study? (formative)
- How will we check for understanding in meaningful ways? How often will we do this?
- What tools will be used to measure performance on the assessments?
- How can we ensure the assessments are reliable?

The overarching goal is to know how learners will show you—and themselves—that they were successful in mastering what you expected them to learn. Educators have many options with which to construct an assessment framework—a plan that outlines the different types of assessment, their purposes, and their frequencies. Consider the constraints of time and technology that impact your choices, and build your framework long before you start designing sessions.

A successful assessment framework serves (at least) two purposes. First, it guides the curriculum designer/instructor to create learning and practices experiences that will lead to success on assessments. Second, it shows learners what to expect as their course unfolds. Strong frameworks include:

- A list of all assessments, formative and summative, included in the course or program.
- Descriptions of each type of assessment, including the mode of evaluation (rubric, peer review, self-reflection, right/wrong responses, etc.).
- Logistical considerations: setting (whether the assessment happens online at a specific moment, or in class), the frequency/schedule of assessments.

Traditional assessment methods such as multiple-choice and short-answer questions will always have a place in classroom learning, yet they do have limitations. They are great options when assessing acquisition of knowledge, and knowledge is the basis of skills. Be mindful not to assume success on knowledge-based assessments indicates mastery of skills. Use knowledge-based assessments as informal checks for understanding that support growth en route to more demonstration-based assessments.

Sometimes creating authentic and novel scenarios is a challenge, especially if your understanding of the role is limited due to capacity constraints or authentic access to professionals in the role. Consider using generative AI to help create role-play scenarios and assessment items. By crafting specific prompts, you can have meaningful and varied first drafts of assessment items or project descriptions that leverage the collective knowledge of incredible data sets and large language models. Generative AI can also help you draft interview questions specific to industries and roles if your course or program features mock job interviews in the syllabus or assessment plan. Again, there is no promise that content and scenarios created by ChatGPT or similar are 100% authentic. Use your best judgment to evaluate what is helpful.

Role-plays and simulations can be used as assessments if performance criteria is shared with learners in advance. Project-based assessments show what students can create and build that is especially useful when learners are creating a work-product portfolio to support an upcoming job hunt. Presentations can also support skills-demonstrations when the targeted skills involve verbal and nonverbal communication.

Figure 9.3 shows a sample assessment framework that is agnostic to a particular role or program.

Assessment	Frequency	Mode	Description
Multiple Choice Quick Quizzes	Once a week, and also at the end of every unit	Automated quiz on LMS	Short, 5-question checks for understanding to gauge acquisition of knowledge
Scored Role-Play	3 times through program	Rubric-based performance in class	Similar to the other role-plays; evaluates 2–3 skills per scored role-play
Unit Assessments	1 per unit (6 total)	Varied based on contents	While mode varies (video submissions, scenario-based simulation . . .), each unit assessment requires 30–60 minutes of preparation outside of class and tests knowledge and skills
Mid-point Assessment	1 time, midway through course	In class—mix of short-answer questions and simulated prompts scored on a rubric	Covers the contents from the first 3 units, including SEL content
Final Project	1 time, at end of course	A group-based performance assessment that combines technical and SEL skills	Requires 3–4 hours of work with a group outside of class as well as a group in-class presentation

Figure 9.3: Sample assessment framework.

In addition to items noted in an assessment framework, teachers are constantly gauging learner mastery through practice and discussions in activities like labs, case studies, drills, and more. The types of practice are dependent on the performance goals and what the job demands. Practice experiences also give instructors multiple opportunities to informally assess learner progress. If the instructor is trained in the specific performance goals and skills needed to be successful, they can better serve as a coach and facilitator of learning, guiding students as they work toward the program's goals.

While making the assessment experience authentic is the overall goal, there are times that you will need to make adaptations. Consider a role where hiring managers prefer (or require) applications with a passing score on a specific industry assessment or certification. It can be difficult to focus both on the industry-vetted skills necessary for success on the job *as well as* the exam preparations and knowledge-based content needed to pass the certification exam. After identifying the job activities, skills, and performance goals, map these factors against the goals of the industry certification and make decisions as to how to augment the learning experience and prepare students to meet the demands of the certification.

This might mean building in practice exam sessions and small teaching bursts that mimic the assessment type. As we said, the multiple-choice format only assesses basic knowledge and is not a great indication of how someone will then perform; yet, it makes great sense to include knowledge-based questions in the assessment framework when they mimic the content and format of the industry certification exam. Multiple-choice questions can also be a quick win for instructors given the speed of scoring, much of which can be automated using today's technology.

Select Employability Skills That Will Be Taught in Addition to the Role's "Hard" Skills

This is the time for your prior—or concurrent—SEL work to shine. Consider the language and frameworks you've put into place with your learners. What connections are easily made between what was learned during your Skills Mapping, Activity Mapping, and other research?

The instructor will teach, model, personalize, practice, and assess student skill development over the course of the program.

The integration of SEL knowledge, skills, and aptitudes will have the greatest impact when integrated into technical sessions in addition to focused sessions, practice opportunities, and assessments. Push yourself to frame SEL and other employability skills using language and planned actions that are framed as objectively as possible. Invest time—including instructor inter-rater reliability training on rubrics or other assessment criteria—to plan for how learners will be assessed on their mastery of these skills. Rubrics are certainly not perfect, but nothing is perfect when you're aiming to evaluate dozens of learners against a skills-mix that goes beyond factual knowledge.

Encourage your learners to consider their own core values—what do they hold dear, and how do they want others to feel when they interact with them? Do they have a core value or social skill they'd like to strengthen based on their research of their targeted roles? Connecting their career preparation to their own desires for personal development can amplify the impact of SEL content. If they haven't done so already, encourage them to connect their core values—or their desired core values—back to the breakdown moment they identified or estimated.

If targeted SEL skills aren't easily identified from limited Activity Mapping or role research for role-based programs, look up core values of companies that hire for this role, or look again at job descriptions for key words and themes. When in doubt, look to the frameworks covered in Chapter 3 and use your best judgment to isolate three to four competencies that would apply to the work.

Some organizations, programs, or school districts will develop committees of industry professionals or gather alumni to understand the experience of recent job hunters. This offers a trove of authentic input and feedback that can affirm or amend the selection of key SEL skills and themes. If this isn't happening in your context, consider if you could benefit from even a few informal conversations with recent graduates or local industry professionals.

There are, to be sure, core values and competencies that transcend roles and industries. Improving communication skills is always worth the effort, even though the style and mode of communication varies greatly between industries and roles. Empathy and compassion for others—be it teammates, customers, managers—is beneficial in endless circumstances. Flexibility and adaptability will continue to be important given the rate of change in our use of technologies like generative

AI. Taking personal responsibility for the success, and shortcomings, of your work—without blaming others—is a trait desired by teams everywhere. If specific SEL skills for a particular role cannot be identified, work from skills you know to be valuable in any context and start there.

In summary, when indicators are clear, follow their lead, and when not clear, use your expertise to select a small number of focused SEL themes that will run through your course or program.

Design an Interactive Learning Journey

Once you have a clear and complete picture of the targeted skills that will be taught and integrated within a unit or training program, it's time to apply the learnings from Activity Mapping to a scope and sequence that will enable building out the program session by session. Keep the intersection of employability/SEL skills and technical skills top of mind as you begin to build session plans.

At this stage, it is time to design a learning journey for the student that will culminate in meeting the performance goals. There are several considerations to determine the overall design of the program (online, blended, or in-person) and the daily schedule (based on learner profile and needs). For each session, start with a description of the session assessment that is aligned to the session objective—always check to make sure these objectives build to the performance goals. Doing so further benefits from the UbD approach highlighted earlier.

Pushing for crisp key points (desired learner takeaways from the session) ensures that the most important, objective-aligned messages do not get lost—that the most salient points land well with learners. The actual flow of the lesson will depend on the lesson type; consider whether it is more student-centered and project-based, whether it is a review of prior content or direct instruction of new material, and whether there is an appropriate balance of teaching new points, modeling, reflecting, discussing, and allowing moments of practice.

If you are expecting to use guidelines and strategies from this chapter to power individual learner explorations of a role, consider what success at the end of their process would be. Are they completing a research project to present to peers? Creating a career plan with actionable next steps for a defined period of time? Are they finding inputs to support a major decision about post-secondary options? Whatever the goal is, help your learners make this concrete by defining success criteria met via scaffolded objectives achieved along the way. Make it clear that you're giving them a process they can follow in the future whenever they find themselves facing a change in career or company.

Whatever the learning experience you are supporting—be it a student-led exploration, a role-specific training program, or something in between—aim to accomplish this through varied types of learner experiences and practice opportunities. Students will benefit from a mix of content. Consider experiences that . . .

- Focus explicitly on SEL and the enduring, essential skills related to a role.
- Mimic real-life scenarios and provide practice moments that are as authentic as possible.
- Require learners to talk and connect.
- Drive learners to be curious and pursue independent research and learning.
- Connect learners to professionals in the field.
- Distinctly cover the processes of finding, applying for, and interviewing for roles.
- Create connections between learners that will endure beyond your classroom to establish the beginnings of a professional network.

Employment at the Center of Design

When Generation brings on a new curriculum designer, it invests over 20 hours of training for onboarding them to its approach. Thereafter, they are partnered with a design buddy for several sessions before drafting content solo for peer and manager review. Even after that rich onboarding and training experience, it often takes a designer several months to fully ramp up to the level of proficient designer. This is to say that employment-focused curriculum design is a skill to be developed and not an automatic or obvious extension of other types of curriculum design. Doing this work well takes practice. Rome wasn't built in a day. Neither was any decent training curricula ever designed.

This chapter gave you a framework for infusing employer needs into curriculum while also attending to the needs of your primary audience—the learner. I hope it's provided ideas and inspiration for refining your own practice as you endeavor to enhance your learners' employability.

I must acknowledge that you, the teacher, are not the sole person responsible for each student's employability outcomes. You must do your best, day in and out, and trust that the rest of the needed puzzle pieces come together to complete the picture for your learners. I also acknowledge that unless you are directing the design of a role-specific career-training curriculum, you're unlikely to follow the full process outlined here step by step.

No one teaches in a vacuum, and all educators and trainers have different levels of control and influence over what and how they teach. Regardless of context, the best educators are creative, ambitious, and laser-focused on outcomes for their learners. To that end:

- While you may not have access to multiple employers or individuals in a particular role, perhaps you can identify one person locally who'd be open to a conversation.
- While you may not have time or access to multiple HR departments, perhaps you and your learners can do a deep dive into multiple job postings to identify common threads and compare listed prerequisites.
- While you may not have control over the performance goals your curriculum pursues, perhaps you can add supplemental targets that reflect what you and your students have discovered.
- While you may not have time to integrate as many types of activities or assessments as you'd like, perhaps you can try one new session or lesson plan when your next semester or cohort begins.

My goal is to inspire you to think deeply about the roles and industries of interest to your learners, and integrate as much authenticity as you can to your preparations and to your students' activities. Teaching is an act of creativity and experimentation. Give yourself permission to dream big, brainstorm with abandon, and try new things.

The curricular approach outlined in this chapter is an essential step in Generation's seven-step education-to-employment methodology that

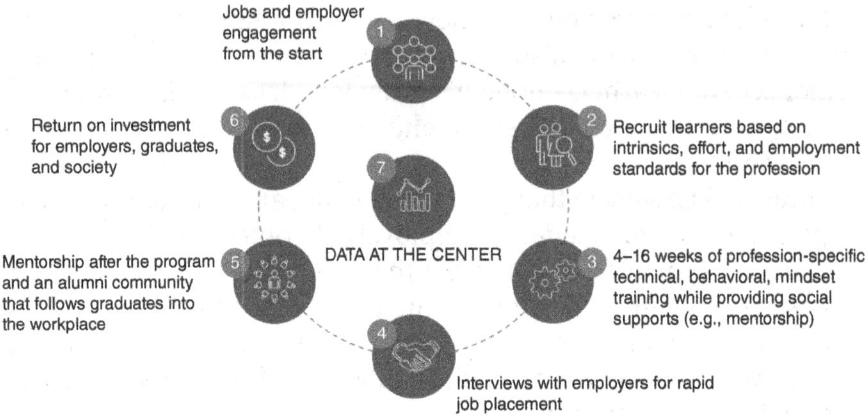

Figure 9.4: Generation's seven-step methodology. The organization is Generation: You Employed.

has brought employment success to many, many learners. The methodology, shown in Figure 9.4, has led to job placement rates of 82% for over 100,000 learners—and counting!—across 17 countries globally. Employers also experience high rates of satisfaction with 92% claiming they would hire graduates again and 82% of employers naming that Generation graduates perform as well as or better than their peers on the job.

I acknowledge I hold bias toward Generation's approach given my time with the organization and the success we've achieved. Yet, I wouldn't include this here were it not for the proven efficacy of this approach. While training alone is not sufficient to place learners into careers, and the total support ecosystem is essential, curriculum and instruction are the most critical levers that educators get to press. We have incredible access to learners at key points in their employment journey, and we must endeavor to make the most of those moments.

A Note on Design Thinking

Innovative schools, programs, and practitioners have of late been applying Design Thinking to curricular design processes. This is a wonderful approach that centers the learner and their needs. It leads with empathy, assuming the best of the end user—in our case, the learner. Curriculum designers have borrowed this approach from non-education sector product designers and innovators who know that a user's experience with a product will make or break its adoption in the marketplace. For those looking for a primer on applying Design Thinking to curriculum design, please see the Resource Guide for suggested content.

Bringing this focus to what a learner needs from both the content and the *experience* learning the content helps increase mastery and engagement. Understanding by Design and Design Thinking can work together to deliver a high-impact curriculum that teachers will love to teach. UbD focuses on the content, and Design Thinking focuses on the learner's journey with that content—they complement each other well when done thoughtfully. Design Thinking also prioritizes rapid iterations and tight feedback loops so that the learner response to the curriculum is highly influential to its end design.

Design Thinking, like UbD, is a framework upon which to hang the targeted goals, objectives, and learning experiences you want to achieve with your learners. If your school or program is encouraging Design Thinking for your curricular planning, be sure to account for your learner's future employability needs as you design, test, and revise.

Reflections and Intentions

- What are two or three ideas that grabbed your imagination as you read this chapter?
- Did any content presented here make you think, "No, that won't work for my situation"? What can you learn from that response? Would you commit to brainstorming a related idea that you could try in your situation?
- How does the curriculum design approach described here compare and contrast to your own approach (if you design curriculum)?

Conclusion

"Let us put our minds together and see what life we can make for our children."

—Sitting Bull

In the fall of 2020, the United States faced a brand-new school year while Covid-19 loomed *large* in our collective consciousness. The school year launched amid great uncertainty, fear, and tension as decisions about virtual versus in-person instruction, exposure protocols, and personal protective equipment required action. Five-year-old children started kindergarten from home in front of computer screens. Athletic programs hung in limbo. Parents moved students from school to school searching for something that worked for their families. Teachers taught entire semesters without ever seeing some of their students' faces. It was a season of tremendous uncertainty and necessary innovation, of boldly doing things in new ways even if we didn't like it, of sacrificing what was comfortable.

By the fall of 2021, we began the school year with Covid-19 still looming, but not quite as large. A return to normalcy felt a bit more possible. Parents, teachers, school boards, administrators, learners—everyone's dreams for the new year had more breathing room now that the pandemic was 18 months old. Educators and stakeholders thought about what was possible more than just what was acceptable.

Secretary of Education Miguel Cardona had been appointed to his position the previous March, almost a year exactly after the World Health Organization declared the novel coronavirus to be a global pandemic. In September 2021, he addressed the nation as educators rolled up their sleeves to reopen the schools. "This is our moment to truly reimagine education," he proclaimed. He believed this moment was a unique opportunity to reset everything—to focus on equity and to support learners disproportionately impacted by the pandemic. He dreamed that we wouldn't simply yearn to return to the way things were before, but that we'd hunger for something better and reach for it together. He told us that, "To elevate our education system to lead the world, we must transform education beyond high school so that it works for everybody, and so that it leads to well-paying, rewarding careers."

Now, several years later, his clarion call still resonates. The intensity of the pandemic's first years is well behind us, but the moment to make a great transformation is still before us. We're sitting at the edge of a wave of innovation, change, and growth, giving us an opportunity to reset and reground in what our students will need near- and long-term. We can let the wave roll over us if we choose. Or we can catch it, hang on tight, and bring our students along for the ride.

We have the power to transform how we think about and facilitate learning experiences that lead to increased employability. It's a necessary shift, though often daunting. The need for this shift doesn't reduce the pressures and requirements you already face. It doesn't negate the core content outlined in your state standards. It doesn't decrease the volume of skills that must be taught before your learners sit for certification exams. It doesn't replace the endless other aspects of your work that draw on your reserves every single day.

I have no magic wand. But in my experiences, both doing the work and supporting others in the work, three themes repeatedly surface. Independently, they are buoys in rough waters offering hope, guidance, and next steps. Together, they provide a potent remedy to the feeling of being overwhelmed, too often faced in this career.

There Is Power in Community

Wherever you are in your journey as a teacher, there once was a day when you were brand-new at this. Situate yourself in a memory from your earliest days. What did it feel like to walk into that classroom? To open the virtual room and admit the learners from the waiting room for the first time? To see the roster of names in your very first class?

In your early days, how did you learn the ropes and make sense of it all? Who did you turn to when you couldn't break through to a learner, or when a directive from an administrator flat out made no sense? For me, it was my fellow teachers. They made the difference between thriving and failing, between hope and despair, and on at least one occasion, between quitting and staying put. I'm betting it was the same for you.

The power that comes by supporting each other through times of growth and change is unlike any other. Mentors, managers, coaches, and visiting consultants all help. They have wisdom and expertise to share, and we are each wise to pay attention and get from them all we can. But leaning on the people beside you every day, the ones doing the same work as you, brings authenticity and accountability that help drive real change.

Consider who else nearby may also want to pursue employability for learners. If you teach in a department, are any of your peers there open to a shift like this? If not, what about the teacher across the hall—the one who teaches something completely different from you? For the virtual educators, your community likely lives online. Wonderful! You don't need a teacher's lounge or an actual water cooler to spur each other on.

In fact, all educators can benefit from online communities, regardless of the courses or programs they teach. Find a virtual meet-up, Reddit thread, or social media group that centers on learner outcomes, jobs of the future, or tech innovations; if something in this book resonated with you, it surely resonated with others, too. Find one another and begin the work together.

Share your intentions. Brainstorm. Plan. Read and research. Listen. Compare frameworks, tools, and sessions that your districts and programs are providing. Listen some more. Celebrate the wins and failures. Shift *together*.

Start Somewhere, and Start Small

Rome wasn't built in a day. A journey of a thousand miles starts with a single step. How do you eat an elephant? One bite at a time.

Got any others?

We have so many adages to describe the fact that you can't do it all at once—that you have to start somewhere. And, of course we do. Such a profound truth needs to find its way into each of our psyches, and adages are nothing if not highly effective little information delivery systems. When considering how you personally will shift your practice toward increased employability for learners, pick whichever adage you like best—but heed the wisdom, and just get started.

I predict there were moments in your reading of this book that made you think, "Well, that's all well and good, but how could I do all that?" I even heard my own inner teacher voice say similar phrases at times as I wrote. But don't let good be the enemy of great. Listen for the small voice that persists, encouraging you to engage and spurring you to action.

- *How can I bring an entire social-emotional learning (SEL) framework or program to my school when we have no money and no capacity for something new?*
    - Start with one lesson in your singular classroom. See where that goes. Free resources abound online; ask your fellow teachers what they've tried. Try just one lesson—then evaluate.
- *Activity Mapping sounds great, but I couldn't possibly be expected to talk to that many employers just to learn about one role. My students all want to pursue different things.*
    - Who's one person you can reach out to that might offer a piece of wisdom or inspiration to your learners? Or, what's one existing project in your syllabus that can be augmented to include a student-led element of Activity Mapping? Is there anything in the process that sparked a new idea for you? Start there and see what comes of it.
- *Program evaluation is important, of course. But there's no way I can mount an entire data collection and evaluation system like that.*
    - That's okay. What do you want to measure around SEL implementation? Maybe just start with learner surveys. Do them once or twice a month. Start with one criterion for success—just one piece of evidence that, if present, would let you know it worked, if even a little bit. After that, see what feels like the best next step.

Shifting your own practice doesn't have to happen within a context of whole school or district-wide implementation. How wonderful if it did! But don't wait for the perfect conditions to land before you to get started. Decide on one goal you can achieve that's new and targeted. Do your work, then step back. Reflect. Repeat.

Everything Begins with Intention

At the end of a yoga class, you may find yourself relaxed, exhausted, sleepy, at peace, sweaty—or most likely, some combination thereof. Whatever your mix of physical and mental feelings in that moment, it's a result of what you accomplished in the class. Chances are good that at the start of class, your teacher offered you an intention, or perhaps invited you to set one for yourself.

The intention you set at the beginning of a yoga class is meant to focus your attention on what you want to achieve in that session. It's a frame on which you can hang the rest of your thoughts throughout your practice. *I am present. I am grounded. I am enough*. These and infinite others help yogis still their minds and focus their energy while practicing their ancient art.

You, too, choose to practice an ancient art every day. There is something deeply human about helping others by teaching them something they need to know to survive. And in the hectic, nonstop blur of modern life, it is easy to miss opportunities to ground yourself in your work and set an intention of how you want your practice to evolve.

Think about what you want to be different in your classroom after reading this book. What would you like to try? What do you want to be true at the end of the month? End of this cohort's program? End of the semester?

- I will promote SEL components, like self-awareness and social awareness, in my learners' lives.
- I will bring the outside in by affirming my learners' experiences outside of my class.
- My colleagues, students, and I will engage with local professionals to bring authentic work scenarios and challenges into our classrooms.
- I will challenge my own thinking about what merits a "good job," especially given the rapidly changing world of work.
- I will look for my students' passions and guide them to nurture and honor what brings them joy.

Again, start small, and harness the power of your teaching community. I half want to launch into a predictable recommendation to turn that intention into a SMART goal, and then advise you to Backwards

Map from that goal to get to your starting point. But you're educators. You've got this.

So, start with an intention—a desire for something to be different and an affirmation that declares it will be so. Water that seed, give it sunshine, and it will grow.

Go Forward

None of us knows what the next several years will bring to the Future of Work, except that change is coming. We want our learners to be ready, to know what might be out there waiting for them, and to develop the knowledge, skills, and traits that will serve them well. We want our teaching to evolve to make this possible. And we have the power to get started.

My whole life has been spent in and near classrooms. I have not taken for granted the privilege that I have had to observe countless teachers in many contexts in the United States and abroad. Watching students learn together, ask questions, and debate one another is always fascinating. Observing teachers hone their craft, try new strategies, and learn alongside students has brought me great joy.

Given the challenges that come with teaching, especially in this current moment, the enduring strength and endless creativity I've witnessed in educators is humbling. You are not celebrated enough. Despite changing political climates, stagnant pay, decreasing classroom autonomy, and tremendous social change, there's so much good already happening in our classrooms.

Take a moment and recognize the incredible work you're doing. Your impact on your students' lives could never be fully measured.

It has been an honor to share this book with you. My hope is that through reading it, you're energized to face the societal changes knocking at our door. To trade anxiety for optimism when thinking of the Future of Work. To embrace disruptive innovation for the betterment of your learners and your practice as an educator.

May your journey forward be as affirming and supportive as the guidance and instruction you offer your students day in and day out. With all that I am, I thank you for what you do, and for embracing the shift toward greater employability for learners, both for today and for the future.

Resource Guide

Resource	Description	URL
Personal Values Card Sort	Activity: Exercise that encourages the participant to prioritize and realize personal values.	https://motivationalinterviewing.org/personal-values-card-sort-instructions
Take a Stand: Human Barometer Activity	Activity: Students have an opportunity to reflect on and share personal values and/or beliefs about social issues and topics of national as well as international concern.	https://amhistory.si.edu/docs/Human_Barometer_Activity.pdf
Active Listening Conversation Partners	Activity: Exercises that allow the learner to practice active listening.	https://blog.trainerswarehouse.com/active-listening-exercises
"Essential Carol Dweck"	Article: There are two main mindsets we can navigate life with: growth and fixed. Having a growth mindset is essential for success.	https://fs.blog/carol-dweck-mindset/
***Atomic Habits* by James Clear**	Book: A comprehensive guide on how to change your habits and get 1% better every day.	https://jamesclear.com/atomic-habits

Resource	Description	URL
***The Upside of Stress* by Kelly McGonigal**	Book: Learn practical strategies for transforming anxiety into courage, isolation into connection, and adversity into meaning.	https://www.penguinrandomhouse.com/books/316675/the-upside-of-stress-by-kelly-mcgonigal/
"Bridging the Gap: Creating a New Approach for Assuring 21st Century Employability Skills" by Ralph Wolff & Melanie Booth	Article: Authors Ralph Wolff and Melanie Booth examine the value of higher education in determining employability.	https://www.tandfonline.com/doi/abs/10.1080/00091383.2017.1399040?journalCode=vchn20
***The Work of the Future* by David Mindell and Elisabeth Reynolds**	Book: A look at why the United States lags behind other industrialized countries in sharing the benefits of innovation with workers, and how we can remedy the problem.	https://mitpress.mit.edu/9780262367745/the-work-of-the-future/
"Defining the Skills Citizens Will Need in the Future World of Work" by Marco Dondi, Julia Klier, Frédéric Panier, and Jörg Schubert	Article: To future-proof citizens' ability to work, new skills will be required—but which ones? A survey of 18,000 people in 15 countries suggests those that governments may wish to prioritize.	https://www.mckinsey.com/industries/public-and-social-sector/our-insights/defining-the-skills-citizens-will-need-in-the-future-world-of-work
LAUNCH	Program model: LAUNCH blends real-world activities with high school curriculum to achieve fantastic results.	https://launch.yourcapsnetwork.org

Resource	Description	URL
Understanding by Design **by Grant Wiggins and Jay McTighe**	Book: Grant Wiggins and Jay McTighe provide an expanded array of practical tools and strategies for designing curriculum, instruction, and assessments that lead students at all grade levels to genuine understanding.	https://files.ascd.org/staticfiles/ascd/pdf/siteASCD/publications/UbD_WhitePaper0312.pdf
The EdTech Center (ETC) at World Education	Organization: World Education's award-winning ETC works with educators, employers, local partners, youth, families, communities, and other system-wide stakeholders in the integration of digital tools and solutions to improve the quality of life and learning outcomes.	https://edtech.worlded.org/our-work/
"5 Myths about Social Emotional Learning" by Amanda Morin	Article: Numerous studies show that SEL builds the foundation for thriving in life—inside and outside the classroom. But there are still misconceptions about SEL. Here are five of the most common myths—with the facts to debunk them.	https://www.understood.org/en/articles/5-myths-about-social-emotional-learning

Resource	Description	URL
Design Thinking for Educators	Toolkit: A new resource—The Co-Designing Schools Toolkit—which supports educators to collaboratively create equitable change in schools through a community-led, equity-centered, and design-driven process.	https://www.ideo.com/post/design-thinking-for-educators
Collaborative for Academic, Social, and Emotional Learning (CASEL)	Organization: CASEL is helping make evidence-based social and emotional learning an integral part of education from preschool through high school.	https://casel.org/
National Association of Colleges and Employers (NACE)	Organization: NACE is the leading source of information on the employment of the college-educated, and forecasts hiring and trends in the job market; tracks starting salaries, recruiting, and hiring practices, and student attitudes and outcomes, and identifies best practices and benchmarks.	https://www.naceweb.org/
Society for Human Resource Management (SHRM)	Organization: SHRM creates better workplaces where employers and employees thrive together. As the voice of all things work, workers, and the workplace, SHRM is the foremost expert,	https://www.shrm.org/

Resource	Description	URL
	convener, and thought leader on issues impacting today's evolving workplaces.	
World Economic Forum (WEF)	Organization: The Forum engages the foremost political, business, cultural, and other leaders of society to shape global, regional, and industry agendas.	https://www.weforum.org/
America Succeeds	Organization: A nonprofit education advocacy organization that engages business leaders in modernizing education systems to drive equity and opportunity. They invite us to join them in transforming the school-to-work pipeline to ensure every child and community can succeed in the competitive global economy.	https://americas-succeeds.org/
***Mindset* by Carol Dweck**	Book: Dweck shows how success in school, work, sports, the arts, and almost every area of human endeavor can be dramatically influenced by how we think about our talents and abilities.	https://www.penguin-randomhouse.com/books/44330/mindset-by-carol-s-dweck-phd/

Resource	Description	URL
***Thanks for the Feedback* by Sheila Heen and Douglas Stone**	Book: Sheila Heen and Douglas Stone cover how to become a better receiver of feedback so that you can improve your job performance and strengthen your personal relationships.	https://openlibrary.org/books/OL27557979M/Thanks_for_the_Feedback
The Mayer-Salovey-Caruso Emotional Intelligence Test (MSCEIT)	Assessment: An ability-based test designed to measure the four branches of the EI model of Mayer and Salovey. MSCEIT was developed from the first published ability measure specifically intended to assess emotional intelligence.	https://www.eiconsortium.org/measures/msceit.html
"Conversations with Kids" from Transcend Education by David Nitkin and Jenee Henry Wood	Article: Results from a 20,000-person-strong survey that sought to learn from children how they felt about learning and school.	https://drive.google.com/file/d/1imWgQhwzdDphycitik4r18IFjmsbjs-w/view
"The Future of Jobs in the Era of AI" by Rainer Strack, Miguel Carrasco, Philipp Kolo, Nicholas Nouri, Michael Priddis, and Richard George	Article: A 2021 look at the impact of automation, artificial intelligence (AI), and other technologies on the global job market.	https://www.bcg.com/publications/2021/impact-of-new-technologies-on-jobs
"A Snapshot of Vocational Education from 1992: How Have Things Changed Today?" by Student Research Foundation	Article: A survey of vocational education from the last 30 years.	https://www.studentresearchfoundation.org/blog/a-snapshot-of-vocational-education/

Resource	Description	URL
"Why 99 Percent of People Choose the Wrong Career Path (and 4 Steps to Get You Back on Track)" by J.T. O'Donnell	Article: A look at why many people feel they are not suited for their careers, and steps to get into a career that fits.	https://www.inc.com/jt-odonnell/why-99-percent-of-people-choose-wrong-career-path-and-4-steps-to-get-you-back-on-track.html
"The Future of Work: Productive Anywhere"	Article: A survey of recent attitudes and approaches to virtual and hybrid work.	https://www.accenture.com/_acnmedia/PDF-155/Accenture-Future-Of-Work-Global-Report.pdf#zoom=40
"How Organizations Can Become Project-Based in the Future of Work" by Yolanda Lau	Article: A guide for organizations to move toward project-based work.	https://www.forbes.com/sites/forbeshumanresourcescouncil/2021/06/02/how-organizations-can-become-project-based-in-the-future-of-work/?sh=5ea4d77729e4
***The Human Skills We Need in an Unpredictable World* by Margaret Heffernan**	Margaret Heffernan shares why we need less tech and more messy human skills—imagination, humility, bravery—to solve problems in business, government, and life in an unpredictable age. "We are brave enough to invent things we've never seen before," she says. "We can make any future we choose."	https://www.ted.com/talks/margaret_heffernan_the_human_skills_we_need_in_an_unpredictable_world
Reboot Foundation	Organization: Its mission is to develop tools and resources to help people cultivate a capacity for critical thinking, media literacy, and reflective thought.	https://reboot-foundation.org/

References

Belfield, C., Bowden, A. B., Klapp, A., Levin, H., Shand, R., & Zander, S. (2015). The economic value of social and emotional learning. *Journal of Benefit-Cost Analysis*, *6*(3), 508–544.

Booth, Barbara. Skilled freelancers, earning more per hour than 70% of workers in US, don't want traditional jobs. *CNBC*, 3 October 2019, https://www.cnbc.com/2019/10/03/skilled-freelancers-earn-more-per-hour-than-70percent-of-workers-in-us.html

Brown, Sara. (2020, July 29). A new study measures the actual impact of robots on jobs. It's significant." MIT Management Sloan School, mitsloan.mit.edu/ideas-made-to-matter/a-new-study-measures-actual-impact-robots-jobs-its-significant

Cardona, M. (2022, January 27). Vision for education in America [speech].

Chetty, R., Jackson, M. O., Kuchler, T., Stroebel, J., Hendren, N., Fluegge, R. B., Gong, S., Gonzalez, F., Grondin, A., Jacob, M., Johnston, D., Koenen, M., Laguna-Muggenburg, E., Mudekereza, F., Rutter, T., Thor, N., Townsend, W., Zhang, R., Bailey, M., . . . , & Wernerfelt, N. (2022). Social capital II: Determinants of economic connectedness. *Nature*, *608*(7921), 122–134, https://doi.org/10.1038/s41586-022-04997-3

Clear, J. M. (2018). *Atomic habits: An easy & proven way to build good habits & break bad ones.* Penguin Random House, https://catalog.umj.ac.id/index.php?p=show_detail&id=62390

Cole, L., Short, S., Cowart, C., & Muller, S. (2021, Oct.). The high demand for Durable Skills [report]. *America Succeeds*, https://americasucceeds.org/wp-content/uploads/2021/04/AmericaSucceeds-DurableSkills-NationalFactSheet-2021.pdf

Corcoran, R. P., Cheung, A. C., Kim, E., & Xie, C. (2018). Effective universal school-based social and emotional learning programs for improving academic achievement: A systematic review and meta-analysis of 50 years of research. *Educational Research Review*, *25*, 56–72.

Corcoran, R. P., O'Flaherty, J., Xie, C., & Cheung, A. C. (2019). Conceptualizing and measuring social and emotional learning: A systematic review and meta-analysis of moral reasoning and academic achievement, religiosity, political orientation, personality. *Educational Research Review, 30*, 100285.

DeSilver, D. (2020, May 30). Most Americans unaware that as U.S. manufacturing jobs have disappeared, output has grown. *Pew Research Center,* https://www.pewresearch.org/short-reads/2017/07/25/most-americans-unaware-that-as-u-s-manufacturing-jobs-have-disappeared-output-has-grown/

Durlak, J.A., Weissberg, R.P., Dymnicki, A., Taylor, R.D., & Schellinger, K.B. (2011). The impact of enhancing students' social and emotional learning: A meta-analysis of school-based universal interventions. *Child Development, 82*, 405–432.

Dweck, C. S. (2007). *Mindset: The new psychology of success.* Ballantine Books.

Gaulden, J., & Gottlieb, A. (2017). The Age of agility: Education pathways for the future of work. *America Succeeds,* https://ageofagility.org/wp-content/uploads/2018/05/Age-of-Agility-Report.pdf

Global Workplace Analytics. (n.d.). Latest telecommuting statistics, https://globalworkplaceanalytics.com/telecommuting-statistics

Goodman, Alissa, et al. (2015). *Social and emotional skills in childhood and their long-term effects on adult life.* Early Intervention Foundation.

Goldberg, J. M., Sklad, M., Elfrink, T. R., Schreurs, K. M., Bohlmeijer, E. T., & Clarke, A. M. (2019). Effectiveness of interventions adopting a whole school approach to enhancing social and emotional development: A meta-analysis. *European Journal of Psychology of Education, 34*(4), 755–782.

Grant, A. (2021). *Think again: The power of knowing what you don't know.* Penguin.

High demand for Durable Skills. (n.d.). https://americasucceeds.org/policy-priorities/durable-skills.

Holzer, H. J. (2022, March 9). Understanding the impact of automation on workers, jobs, and wages. *Brookings.* Retrieved August 13, 2022, from https://www.brookings.edu/blog/up-front/2022/01/19/understanding-the-impact-of-automation-on-workers-jobs-and-wages/

Joseph, D. L., Jin, J., Newman, D. A., & O'Boyle, E. H. (2015). Why does self-reported emotional intelligence predict job performance? A meta-analytic investigation of mixed EI. *Journal of Applied Psychology, 100*(2), 298.

Kamarck, Elaine, et al. (2022, March 9). What we know about career and technical education in high school. *Brookings,* www.brookings.edu/articles/what-we-know-about-career-and-technical-education-in-high-school/

Kirkpatrick, James D., & Kayser Kirkpatrick, W. (2016). *Kirkpatrick's four levels of training evaluation.* ATD Press.

Lau, Yolanda. (2021, June 2). Council post: How organizations can become project-based in the future of work. *Forbes,* www.forbes.com/sites/forbeshumanresourcescouncil/2021/06/02/how-organizations-can-become-project-based-in-the-future-of-work/?sh=612ce39e29e4

Mayer, J. D., Caruso, D. R., & Salovey, P. (1997). Emotional intelligence meets traditional standards for an intelligence. *Intelligence, 27*(4), 267–298.

MBO Partners. The great realization: New data shows dramatic surge in freelance workers. *MBO Partners*, 18 Oct. 2021, https://www.mbopartners.com/blog/press/the-great-realization-new-data-shows-dramatic-surge-in-freelance-workers/

McKinsey & Company. (2012). Education to employment: Designing a system that works. McKinsey & Company. Retrieved from https://www.mckinsey.com/~/media/mckinsey/industries/public%20and%20social%20sector/our%20insights/education%20to%20employment%20designing%20a%20system%20that%20works/education%20to%20employment%20designing%20a%20system%20that%20works.pdf

Muenks, K., Canning, E. A., LaCosse, J., Green, D. J., Zirkel, S., Garcia, J. A., & Murphy, M. C. (2020). Does my professor think my ability can change? Students' perceptions of their STEM professors' mindset beliefs predict their psychological vulnerability, engagement, and performance in class. *Journal of Experimental Psychology: General, 149*(11), 2119–2144.

National Association of Colleges and Employers. (2021). Career competencies for a career-ready workforce, https://www.naceweb.org/uploadedfiles/files/2021/resources/nace-career-readiness-competencies-revised-apr-2021.pdf

National Center for Education Statistics. (2021). COE—Public high school graduation rates. National Center for Education Statistics (NCES), a part of the U.S. Department of Education, https://nces.ed.gov/programs/coe/indicator/coi/high-school-graduation-rates

National Women's Law Center. (2022). The economic status of women during the COVID-19 pandemic, https://nwlc.org/wp%20content/uploads/2022/07/UPDATED_JULY2022_NWLC_CovidReport.pdf

Sklad, M., Diekstra, R., Ritter, M. D., Ben, J., & Gravesteijn, C. (2012). Effectiveness of school-based universal social, emotional, and behavioral programs: Do they enhance students' development in the area of skill, behavior, and adjustment? *Psychology in the Schools, 49*(9), 892–909.

Society for Human Resource Management (SHRM). (2022, April 26). What is meant by "the future of work"? Society for Human Resource Management, https://www.shrm.org/ResourcesAndTools/tools-and-samples/Pages/default.aspx

Stahl, A. (2022, September 2). Say goodbye to the 9 to 5: How to master the gig economy. Forbes.com, https://www.forbes.com/sites/

ashleystahl/2022/09/02/say-goodbye-to-the-9-to-5-how-to-master-the-gig-economy/?sh=2771eaf35cd6

Taylor, R. D., Oberle, E., Durlak, J. A., & Weissberg, R. P. (2017). Promoting positive youth development through school-based social and emotional learning interventions: A meta-analysis of follow-up effects. *Child Development*, *88*(4), 1156–1171.

The impact of parental influence: Career Edition. (2021, September 21). Job list.com, https://www.joblist.com/trends/the-impact-of-parental-influence-career-edition

Vast new study shows a key to reducing poverty: More friendships between rich and poor. (2022, August 2). *New York Times—Breaking News, US News, World News, and Videos*, https://www.nytimes.com/interactive/2022/08/01/upshot/rich-poor-friendships.html

Watts, T.W., Gandhi, J., Ibrahim, D.A., Masucci, M.D., & Raver, C.C. (2018). The Chicago School Readiness Project: Examining the long-term impacts of an early childhood intervention. PLoS ONE *13*(7), e0200144, https://doi.org/10.1371/ journal.pone.0200144

What is the CASEL Framework? (2022, September 2). Casel.org, https://casel.org/fundamentals-of-sel/what-is-the-casel-framework/

Wigelsworth, M., Lendrum, A., Oldfield, J., Scott, A., Ten Bokkel, I., Tate, K., & Emery, C. (2016). The impact of trial stage, developer involvement and international transferability on universal social and emotional learning programme outcomes: A meta-analysis. *Cambridge Journal of Education*, *46*(3), 347–376.

Wolff, R., & Booth, M. (2017). Bridging the gap: Creating a new approach for assuring 21st century employability skills. *Change*, *49*(6), 51–54, https://doi-org.cyrano.ucmo.edu/10.1080/00091383.2017.1399040

World Economic Forum. The future of jobs report 2023. (2023, April 30). *World Economic Forum*, https://www.weforum.org/reports/the-future-of-jobs-report-2023/in-full?_gl=1*eadw7i*_up*MQ..&gclid=CjwKCAjwx_eiBhBGEiwA15gLN8vU0nYvxsuQ7KqYYXy

Acknowledgments

FROM KELLY AND DANA:

Thank you to the world-changing brain trust known as the Generation Curriculum and Instruction team. Your fingerprints are everywhere in this book—especially you, Shalini Dwivedi. Your laser focus on excellent instruction is changing the game. And Jenny, you do the steady work of sorting out all the pieces and gluing them together. Your after-hours support on this book was no exception. Thank you, both.

The CEO and Founder of Generation, Dr. Mona Mourshed, cares deeply about the growth and development of her team and is constantly making way for opportunities that will push us beyond our currently capabilities to achieve new heights. Thank you, Mona, for your constant support of not just us, but for education and opportunities for all people.

To our colleagues in the field whose insights have added depth and color to the realities and strategies—namely, Gideon Murenga, Richard Bowden, Robert Hall, Casey Lamb, Alana Zangl, Rajinder Gill, Patrick Perez, Nicola Thomas, and Ebony Tyler.

FROM KELLY:

Writing a book on top of work and family responsibilities is no small feat. I am forever grateful to my husband, Michael Cassaro, who made the time available to me by taking on many additional responsibilities, taking our kids away for the weekend so I could write, and encouraging me when I needed it the most. My sister, Erin Terpack has always paved the way for me to achieve my dreams and I am forever grateful for her guidance and strength.

Special thanks to Dana Lee, who came into this after a rough first draft and provided the support needed to bring it to the hands of our readers. Her writing craft is excellent and her ability to connect to the reader is unmatched. This book is just the very beginning!

I am incredibly grateful to my extended family and supportive friends who never think any goals are too big for me to tackle and serve as my sounding board and encouragement constantly. My children James and Grace are my "why", and I am just in awe of the beautiful people they are and how they constantly encourage me to improve my own essential life skills.

FROM DANA:

Thank you, Kelly, for the challenge and honor of working on this book together. It was an unexpected and rewarding journey that I'll always remember with a smile.

Thank you to the ladies of WIHG—Jenn Woodruff, Lauren Hopkins Karcz, Maryann Dabkowski, Rachael Stewart Allen, and Terra Elan McVoy. Your writerly support and abiding friendship kept me going in even the latest of late nights. Hens before pens! Thank you as well to Gilly Segal and Stephen Lee for your insider knowledge and generous hearts.

Thank you, Caroline and Ada, for the snuggles and laughter and constant reminders that the future is coming fast. And thank you, Nick. Sorry about all the late nights, missed bedtimes, and forsaken Saturdays. Your support, patience, and grace made this all possible. I love you.

About the Authors

Kelly Cassaro is a global learning leader, board member, and advisor. Kelly has over 20 years of experience across various educational contexts as a classroom teacher in New York City public schools, staff developer, recruiter, and chief academic officer. Kelly holds a master's in educational leadership from Bank Street School of Education and a Bachelor of Education from Ohio Wesleyan University. She is passionate about scalable innovation within the education-to-employment ecosphere as well as online learning practices, closing the digital divide, and preparing for the Future of Work. She currently serves as Chief of Learning at Generation, the world's largest education-to-employment organization that has supported over 100,000 learners and counting into careers that would otherwise be inaccessible. Kelly can be found cooking and traveling with her husband and two children.

Dana Lee is the Global Director of Curriculum and Instruction: Product Development at Generation, a global nonprofit organization dedicated to workforce development. She holds a B.A. in French and English from Albion College and a M.Ed. in Learning and Teaching from the Harvard Graduate School of Education. She spent a decade teaching English in the Atlanta Public Schools, getting her start there through Teach For America. She spends her time writing stories, singing in a band with her husband, and chasing their two creative, hilarious daughters around the house.

Index

Page numbers followed by *f* refer to figures